THE HEART OF THE JOURNEY

An Invitation to Healing and Wholeness through
a Relationship of Intimacy with God

Beverly Peterson

ISBN: 979-8-9912844-0-0
ISBN: 979-8-9912844-1-7
ISBN: 979-8-9912844-2-4
ISBN: 979-8-9912844-3-1

Independently Published; 1 edition (November 26, 2024).
Bonita, California 91902

For all who seek a more intimate relationship with God, one in which you are fully known and deeply loved, and by whom you have been divinely created: This book is for you.

And for those who experienced a difficult childhood that left you wondering if healing and wholeness were even possible. They are—and this book is dedicated to you.

And to those who are weary, burnt out on religion, and ready for a real rest and the refreshment and renewal only God can give: the invitation to you is,

"Come."

CONTENTS

PRAISE FOR THE HEART OF THE JOURNEY

The Book

I always want to learn from someone's life work, particularly if that learning can shape my own spiritual journey. That's what Beverly Peterson's book feels like while reading: learning from a master who has put in decades of practice to develop practical ideas and tools for healing and transformation that go well beyond the simplistic or cliché. — **Mark Oestreicher**, *speaker, author, founder of The Youth Cartel*

From the very start I felt myself being immersed in the warm waters of a deep love allowing my pains, griefs, confusions and weariness to be washed, rested, and healed. Beverly's generous heart, formed through her wounds, the vacancies of love and security in her own upbringing, and transformed by a life long-lived in the presence of God allows her to be the perfect guide for us on this journey of our own transformation and healing. She reminds us that "God uses the pain and suffering of our lives to spiritually form us," and shows us how to directly enter into the love and presence of God where all healing takes place. — **Beth Allen Slevcove**, *hospice chaplain, spiritual director, and author of* Broken Hallelujahs: Learning to Grieve the Big and Small Losses of Life

God is always inviting us to MORE depth, intimacy, and soul satisfaction in relationship with Himself. Without a vision for the beauty of what is possible for us as Christ followers, we often find ourselves prey to addictions, hopelessness, and fear. Beverly leads us through a journey of envisioning all that God has to offer, identifying the barriers that keep us from accessing the fullness of life with Him and engaging in practices that guide us to wholeness and healing. I highly recommend The Heart of the Journey as a tool for discipleship and mentoring as well as the road to move beyond what each one of us even thought possible in our experience of life with God. Invest in the journey! You won't regret it! —**Linda Noble**, *Author of* Before the Sex Talk: A Theology of the Body Approach for Parents and Mentors *and Discipleship Director at Journey Community Church, La Mesa, CA*

This phenomenal book is filled with many engaging spiritual practices that draw one into an intimate relationship with God. Beverly's heartwarming stories reveal how God heals our wounds created by life, slowly transforming us into our authentic, true selves. Engaging in this journey will gently create a heart full of love, joy, and peace along with the freedom to be the person God created you to be. **— Anne Richardson**, *spiritual director and author of* Not Alone: Transforming Trauma and Accompanying Survivors

Beverly shares her personal journey towards wholeness and friendship with Jesus in a way that empowers me to make space to know myself and my creator more authentically. I am encouraged and emboldened to follow her lead, and pleased that others will have that opportunity as well. **—Jennevieve LaHaye,** *Spiritual Formation class facilitator, Heart of the Journey small group leader*

The Heart of the Journey is a must-read for anyone seeking a more intimate, abundant relationship with God, and with a willingness to come into the fullness of who we are in relationship to Him. Bev's powerful, transparent, and often vulnerable storytelling from her own lived experience breathes life into the valuable teachings and practices embedded in each of the chapters, making them both relatable and applicable. This book is an ideal and insightful textual companion that will serve as a roadmap for followers hungry for a deeper understanding of God, not only for the seasoned disciple, but for those taking their first steps on the journey towards wholeness and spiritual transformation. – **Barbara Cope**, *MAT, MSW, LCSW*

PRAISE FOR HEART OF THE JOURNEY

The Original Class

I was blessed to take this walk with Bev as my teacher and mentor. I had the privilege of attending and working alongside Beverly Peterson in multiple Heart of the Journey classes. It led me to a deeper and more purposeful walk with God. She used centuries-old and uniquely crafted spiritual practices to give me a framework to understand myself and God at a deeper level. **— Bryan Toth,** *Heart of the Journey tech team leader*

*I took the Heart of the Journey class with Bev at the beginning of my understanding of Spiritual Formation. Already a believer with a strong intimate relationship with Jesus, and a solid foundation in doctrine and theology, this class introduced me to the possibilities of creating space to experience Jesus in new ways. As I learned spiritual practices and ways to enjoy my relationship with God and myself in creative and imaginative ways, I grew and had new skills to continue joyfully loving and living life with God. – **Rikah Thomas,** artist, Biblical counselor, life/writing coach and author of* God Church and Me

Attending Heart of the Journey was empowering and life-changing! I learned how deeply and unconditionally God loves us. Through the Prayer of Examen, I was able to trust the process of being vulnerable with God and with others on the journey with me. **— Becky Toth,** *Heart of the Journey small group leader*

The Heart of the Journey changed my life! What started out as learning regular exercises for healing my mind, became the wonderful pursuit of a joyful heart. Discover Jesus as your joy, too! **—Kathryn Trainor,** *Spiritual formation class facilitator, small group leader*

Heart of the Journey helped me connect with God in ways I had never experienced growing up in church. It allowed me to better embrace God's unconditional love and acceptance in deeper and truer ways. **— Kevin Carlin,** *Heart of the Journey small*

group leader

I was at a place in my spiritual journey where I felt a lack of zeal and excitement about my faith. I was encouraged by a mentor to join the Spiritual Practices group at my church led by Beverly and her husband, ElRoy. Drawing from Scripture, tradition, and her appreciation for the arts, Beverly's kinesthetic teaching methods and spiritual formation practices nudged me from a surface-level faith into a realm where I was more receptive to interacting with the Spirit of God. It's no wonder that those who take her workshops and classes often return again and again. Engaging with these practices gives us a taste of the fullness of life with God and our journey toward wholeness. **— Damian Ludwig,** *Graphic Designer*

INTRODUCTION

Even a Child

I never expected what I was about to experience, as I pulled up in front my son Zack's house After a warm greeting and exchanging a few brief pleasantries, Zack informed me that his then seven-year-old son wanted to share something with me, privately. My son led me to Isaiah's bedroom and then left, closing the door behind him.

"What's up?" I asked Isaiah.

My grandson, Isaiah, shifted a bit on his feet, then he slowly and with some trepidation began to unravel a recent personal story. I stood spellbound as he shared in a low thoughtful voice.

"My mom took me to a Bible study with some of her friends. It was in Balboa Park. We met up by the flower garden. Then we put our chairs in a circle on the grass. We read some Bible verses about forgiveness."

"Was that hard for you?" I asked. "I know you don't always feel comfortable reading out loud in a group."

"It was easy! We all read together."

"Oh, that's great!" I responded.

"Lisa was the leader of the group," Isaiah continued, "and she was having us pray about forgiveness. She told us to think about anyone who had hurt us this week and pray about forgiving them. If we forgave them, we should put our smooth rocks in the bowl of water with the fountain on top. I remembered two kids who were rude to me at school last week."

"What did they do?" I asked, hoping my warm cheeks weren't revealing the concealed anger rising up within me, hearing someone had been rude to him.

"They said some really mean things that hurt my feelings." Isaiah continued, "Lisa told us to take a smooth rock, from her bucket, for each person we wanted to forgive. She said I should pray on my own, and if I was ready, to forgive them. So, then I prayed and forgave them.

"I put my smooth rocks in the bowl of water. It was like a little fountain.

"So, I was sitting on a bench waiting for my mom to be done. She was still praying. I was looking at a green tree, right in front of me. It had some brown dead leaves on it. While I was staring at it, I saw two dead leaves fall off the tree at the same time.

"Then, I felt like God was saying to me that I was like that tree. I was like the tree because even though I had bad feelings about the boys, I could let them go—just like the tree let go of its dead leaves."

Up to this point, I had been mostly listening quietly and respectfully, but my curiosity was piqued, so I asked, "How did God speak to you? Did you actually hear His voice?"

"No, I just knew it inside. I knew what He was saying," Isaiah responded.

In my heart of hearts, I understood what he meant. I had experienced that same "inner knowing."

"That's AWESOME!" I responded, smiling and thinking, "...and a little child shall lead them" (Isaiah 11:6b, ESV).

God had spoken to this seven-year-old boy in a clear, precise way that made an unforgettable connection between God and him. There was absolutely no doubt in his mind or in mine that it truly was God speaking to him.

Overjoyed and honored that Isaiah would share such a personal story with me, I put both arms around him, thanking him for the gift of this very beautiful story of connection with his Heavenly Father.

How kind and compassionate is our God!

Pause And Consider:

Are there times when you've heard God speaking directly to you? Maybe it was a gentle prompting, an audible voice, an impression, or an inner knowing.

Do you long for a more intimate relationship with Him?

What do you most desire from God these days?

Could it be the answers to your deepest questions, freedom from painful childhood memories, spiritual growth, emotional healing, a greater awareness of His love for you?

My prayer for you is that as you read through the pages of this book, you will discover your personal pathway toward the fulfillment of your greatest desires.

The *Heart of the Journey* is a pathway upon which our hearts come to experientially know and become more in tune with God's heart through an intimate friendship with Him.

Welcome To *The Heart Of The Journey*!

May God draw you, empower you, and deepen your relationship with Him.

Increased joy and fulfillment come from knowing and walking with Jesus as your friend and companion. However, God may require exchanging a heart full of brokenness and false beliefs for the priceless gifts of abiding love and friendship.

Following the path to wholeness is an intentional, lifelong process. We sometimes refer to it as the "slow work of God." This path is fraught with questions and challenges as it leads you through the ongoing discovery and a deeper understanding of the presence of our compassionate creator.

Spiritual practices provide space along the way through which we learn to sense God's loving presence more easily and hear Him speaking to us more clearly. A few of these include: prayer, journaling, and a variety of listening practices and tools we use to develop a kind of two-way conversation with God.

Through spiritual practices, we explore ways of being more confident of His love and more aware of His presence within the context of our personal relationships, as well as in the comings and goings of everyday life. We learn to trust God with the most pressing concerns of our hearts.

So, what does a deeper connection with Jesus produce in our hearts and lives?

- We learn how to slow down, lean in, and let Him restore and strengthen our exhausted, anxious hearts.
- We begin to discover our true identity as He shows us how beautifully and uniquely He created us.
- We learn to authentically live out our life's purpose as His beloved.
- His presence heals our souls.
- Consequently, we mature spiritually and our faith is made strong.

A Dance Of The Heart

Throughout my own journey, God's tender presence often encouraged and enlightened me along my path of spiritual discovery. I was swept up into beautiful moments of communion with Him as I prayed and tuned in to His still, small voice.

It felt like a beautiful dance we enjoyed together – a dance of the heart. There were no words, only gentle movements where He neither pushed nor pulled, but gently guided me along the path toward deeper and deeper communion with Him. With Jesus as lead dancer, together we glided across the dance floor in almost effortless motion. These intimate moments brought clarity to what God was doing in me, personally, to heal childhood wounds.

This is the hope I have for you, too: that as I share stories of my own personal life and spiritual journey, you will be drawn toward a deepening desire for more of God. In each chapter you will find encouragement, insights, practical tools, and spiritual exercises so that you, dear reader, can learn to access God's love and grow spiritually. As you grow in intimacy with Him, He will transform you from the inside out, giving you more and more of His character. As a result, you will reflect God's love and, as an outpouring of that love, serve others as He empowers you. Over time you will become more like Him and be inspired to live out His purposes in your life and the world.

For those who have lived through unpredictable, dysfunctional family dynamics or traumatic life experiences, working toward intimacy with God may require additional insight and support. You may find it helpful to reach out to a trusted friend, counselor, spiritual director, pastor, or small group with whom you can process what you are learning and experiencing on this journey. The path toward healing and wholeness is lined with helpful, encouraging companions. Even for those who've grown up in a healthy family dynamic, transformation is meant to be a communal work.

Pause for a moment and consider who you might want to reach out to for support along the path.

When I sensed God calling me, it was explicit and profound, and it shook me to the core! This experience changed the entire direction of my life. He entreated, *"Come away with Me and I will give you rest"* (Matthew 11:28-30). It was a personal invitation with a clear call, but what would come next was not clear at all. I had no idea what the road ahead might require of me, but I had an inner assurance that God desired to do something healing and transformative with the emptiness I felt, and my lifetime of longing to be loved simply for who I was. I hungered for more of God and His healing power, so whatever the cost, I was all in. I said *yes* to leaning into Him in complete trust.

As the process unfolded, ever so gently, Jesus invited me to come closer and to spend more quality time with Him—to rest, to just *be* with Him, and to enjoy His presence.

Coming to *experientially* know God for who He truly is as the lover of my soul, and embracing my true identity, took time and intention. The process began in 1991, in my mid-forties, when I began meeting with my first spiritual director, Natalie, who I would meet with for the next 17 years. Spiritual Formation became the focus of my life for the next thirty years. In the process, I exchanged my false beliefs about God for an understanding of God's true character. Simultaneously, I learned how God saw me, and I began to live out of the knowledge of my true belovedness.

As you become more and more whole, your faith and confidence in God and in yourself will increase. You will be more equipped to live out your God-given purpose, making a positive difference in the world around you.

> *True godliness does not turn us away from hurting, bleeding humanity. Rather it enables us to live fully alive in the midst of human need and enlivens our abilities to bring a healing presence to the bruised and broken around us.*
> *—Richard J. Foster, Celebration of Discipline[1]*

How Did The Heart of the Journey Come to Be?

God's prompting came clearly during my Sunday morning time alone with Him. It wasn't an audible voice, but it was unmistakably His, prompting me to write a class for those desiring to go deeper with Him. The possibility of writing and teaching such a class excited me to my core. I couldn't wait to discuss it with Ann, one of our ministry leaders. I hoped she would be as thrilled as I was.

Upon entering the church lobby, I could see Ann at our Quiet Time booth. I rushed toward her.

"I have some news for you!" I excitedly stated.

"So do I. Me first!" she quickly responded. "During one of my quiet times this week I heard God say He wanted you to write an advanced class for those ready for more of God.

My eyes widened in surprise. I was stunned speechless that we had both gotten almost identical messages from God in the same week. What a profound confirmation

"I've already spoken to the pastor and it's been approved," Ann explained, "so you can begin whenever you're ready."

Unable to contain my astonishment, I blurted out, "That's what I was going to tell you! Just this morning I heard God say almost the exact same thing to me!"

We were both genuinely thrilled, and I planned to move forward with the project.

I had just completed my second year of training to become a Spiritual Director and had so much I wanted to share from all I had learned.

Writing the curriculum, developing the syllabus, and training our team took approximately a year. We advertised our eight-week class plus a full-day contemplative retreat and collected the names of interested people. Then we were ready to begin with close to 100 sign-ups. That first morning as

I stood in front of a room filled with eager learners, the enthusiasm felt electric. This excitement continued through the entire eight-week class and the Saturday retreat.

Participant reviews were overwhelmingly positive, with many reporting that their lives had been changed. One young man in his late 30s told us that he had, for the first time in his life, actually felt God's loving presence and acceptance during an Imaginative Prayer Practice. Even before the class was over, he began teaching others in his small group at church how to do some of the practices.

A second man made an appointment with our pastor, explaining that he had learned exciting new ways of connecting intimately with God he had never before experienced. "I've attended church most of my life, but using these practices we've learned has revolutionized my quiet times with God," he said.

A third man, in his early 50s, came up to me after the third classes. He was tall with dark brown hair, a gentle sort of guy. He thanked me for teaching the class, which he said he had enjoyed so very much.

"I'd like to share something," he stated with reticence.

"Of course," I replied, curious.

"Three weeks ago, before this class began, I was contemplating suicide. I was at the lowest place, emotionally, I'd ever been. When I heard about your class I decided to give it a try. *This will be my last effort to make sense of my life*, I told myself. Right from the start of the very first class, I sensed God speaking to me and drawing me to Him. I felt hope for the first time in a long time. Through this class, God has given me a reason to live again!"

It was a humbling experience, standing with this man as he shared so vulnerably. After a few weeks he asked to join our ministry, and he remained with the ministry for about six years. He is now happily married and doing quite well.

Subsequent classes all reflected similar results. I continued to fine-tune the curriculum and our teaching approach. My husband, ElRoy and I, along with our supportive team, taught Heart of the Journey for the next ten years. We walked alongside those who wanted a more interactive relationship with the divine, encouraging and equipping them to enjoy a fuller, freer life of intimacy with Jesus.

This very effective class has now become a book. My hope is that *The Heart of the Journey* will make its way into the hands and hearts of those ready for an exciting adventure toward spiritual wholeness, healing, and maturity.

Get ready to enjoy the journey!

HOW TO GET THE MOST OUT OF THIS BOOK

Welcome to The Heart of the Journey, a book focused on developing a relationship of intimacy with God, which has the potential to lead you toward personal healing and spiritual transformation. Over the years it has become clear to me that being transformed into the image of God has so much to do with how we understand who God is experientially. Once we develop a well-rounded, true image of who God really is, we can come into God's presence freely and authentically. Another natural outcome of gaining a truer image of God is that we begin to understand how He sees us.

Living out of our true selves requires knowing and embracing all of who we are; one our best days and our worst days.

The first two chapters of this book explain what spiritual formation is and how it happens. Chapters three through six focus on our spiritual growth and maturity, while engaging in a trust relationship with God and developing an accurate view of God and ourselves. Chapters seven to 10 focus on the purpose of the spiritual disciplines or practices, the importance of forgiveness, and strategies for incorporating these practices into a life-giving rhythm. The final chapter encourages us to celebrate God's goodness in large and small evidences of His presence and stay open to the wonder and mystery of God. This focus helps maintain a relationship with God that is fresh and vital and opens us to a life lived in harmony with God and His purposes for us.

Each chapter of *The Heart of the Journey* is divided into several sections. Below are tips and suggestions for how you might read and apply each section effectively.

Tools and Supplies You'll Need

JOURNAL: This workbook includes lines for journaling and answering questions. You may prefer to use a separate journal.

WRITING UTENSILS: Have a pen handy. You might also like to use colored pencils or thin colored markers and a highlighter.

BIBLE: Having a version of the Bible you love might be helpful in case you'd like to refer back to the entire chapter a certain quote is taken from.

My Personal Stories

As you read personal stories, taken mostly from my own life experience, as well as a few from people I have worked with, I invite you to view each one through the wide-angled lens of your own personal camera, as though you were there with me watching the scenes unfold. Grab a front-row seat to the ups and downs, the pain and the ecstasy of God's grace being worked out in my life.

I share parts of my own personal journey with the hope that it will encourage and enlighten your own journey. Some of the stories are glorious glimpses of God's grace revealed in beautifully unique ways. Others are raw, honest examples of life struggles. A few of the stories highlight the causes of my deeply wounded childhood. Every story offers hope to the reader.

My prayer is that each chapter will prompt within you a desire to lean more completely into Jesus and ask Him to personally meet the deepest desires of your heart. Since God is already intimately acquainted with each of us individually, we can learn to trust Him to meet us in the ways that are most suited to each of our unique life journeys.

Questions To Ponder, Journal, And Share

Learning to reflect on and process what we have just learned, read, or experienced is important to personal transformation. A lot of wasted time can be spent going through the motions of mindlessly doing an exercise. Unless we slow down enough to ponder, journal, and share our thoughts and personal insights, much of what we read is forgotten and never applied to our lives. On the other hand, our processing of the information will, most likely, inform our ability to live life more fully, freely, and passionately.

Scripture Passages

In my own journey of healing and transformation, probably the most influential factors have been reading, studying, memorizing, and meditating on passages of Scripture. When God first spoke to me about being transformed, He spoke very specifically about verse two in Romans chapter 12: *"Do not conform to the pattern of this world, but be transformed by the renewing of your mind."*

Much of the process of renewing my mind has come through saturating it with the truth of Scripture. It's through the Bible that we learn who God is: how He thinks, the kinds of things He does, and how He names us. I have spent years grounding my thinking and my beliefs about God's personhood as portrayed in the pages of the Holy Bible. The Sacred Scriptures have illuminated my understanding of how He sees me as a whole, unconditionally loved person.

Old tapes, old messages, and negative labels have been replaced with the truth of God's own words. As I read Scripture, I have found it most helpful to read and reread a short passage very slowly, looking for God's specific message to me. In the case of a story about Jesus, I sometimes read, reread, and picture the story in my mind's eye to see how I might fit in and how I might experience Jesus with me today. It's a way of S-L-O-W-I-N-G down, making space to be with and hear from God. I also find space to be with my own thoughts and discern what I need to authentically bring to God for understanding and healing.

Spiritual Practice Or Discipline?

Christian maturity requires intention. We don't just drift into holiness or growth automatically. Both effort and intention are required. A practice or discipline may not seem comfortable or easy at first. (I use the words "practice" and "discipline" interchangeably.) Disciplines or practices are things we do repeatedly to make space for and to cooperate with God's action in our lives. When I first learned to ride a bike, it was awkward. I was constantly afraid of tipping over. Thankfully, my grandfather's strong hands held the back of my seat to steady me, until I could balance on my own. Over time, peddling and balancing became easier and more natural. The same is true for spiritual practices; they usually become more pleasant and helpful the more we practice them.

There is a wide variety of spiritual practices that can help lead us into the intimate, healing presence of God. These practices help us *slow down* and *make space* for Him to do the work of transforming us. Spiritual practices are a way of being with God and giving Him access to our hearts. They are tools in our toolbox that help move us to a place of surrender so that God can do His miraculous work in us. Spiritual Formation is not *just* about the practices; however, they are *key* to our formation process and are incorporated into every chapter.

Because we are each unique in both personality and needs, some practices may seem easier or more appealing to you. It's important, though, that we engage in both practices that come easily and those that are more challenging in order to grow in a spiritually well-rounded way.

Spiritual practices help us intentionally:
- **Connect with God** (all of the practices)
- **Slow down and give God quality space in our lives** (nature walks, sitting by the beach, Lectio Divina, Imaginative Prayer)
- **Know God more deeply** (Scripture meditation, contemplation)
- **Pay attention to what God is doing** (noticing, Prayer of Examen, Scripture meditation)
- **Process what God is doing in us** (journaling, Prayer of Examen, listening)
- **Become more pliable in God's hands** (surrender, meditation, contemplation, retreat)

Each of the above spiritual practices is mentioned and explained in the chapter called "The Purpose of the Practices."

Spiritual practices are not the goal. They don't transform us in and of themselves, and they are not the only means through which transformation occurs. God also uses the pain and suffering of our lives to spiritually form us—more about this in the chapters to come. Spiritual practices are a means to a desired end; helping us develop a relationship of surrender to our Good Shepherd. Even in the midst of pain and suffering, we can experience the Spirit's nearness. Spiritual disciplines help us become the kind of person God is able to communicate with and communicate through. As we grow in our experience of God's love, we become more comfortable seeing ourselves as God sees us. We are more capable of loving God, others, and even ourselves, as we grow in our personal experience of Divine Love.

Personal Reflections

Reflecting on a practice, an activity, or a story helps us deepen their positive effects in our lives. Without reflection, we might spend time doing a practice without really personalizing it or learning from it. Reflection S-L-O-W-S us down so we can benefit more from the effort we've expended by engaging in an activity.

Extending The Learning

This section of the book offers additional ideas, insights, and suggestions for ways you might want to deepen the learning process. It provides options for an even more thoughtful, thorough look at the topic and how it applies personally to you. You never have to complete all of the suggestions. Choose those that seem most relevant to you or that meet your current needs.

Nuggets For The Journey

Small morsels of wisdom in the form of prayers, poems, and short stories are presented here. I trust they will touch your heart and offer encouragement for the days and weeks ahead. Each nugget will provide something to ponder, pray over, to help cement the concepts, or offer a glimpse of beauty that brings solace for your heart and soul along the journey.

1 THE GRAND INVITATION

A Personal Call To Spiritual Transformation

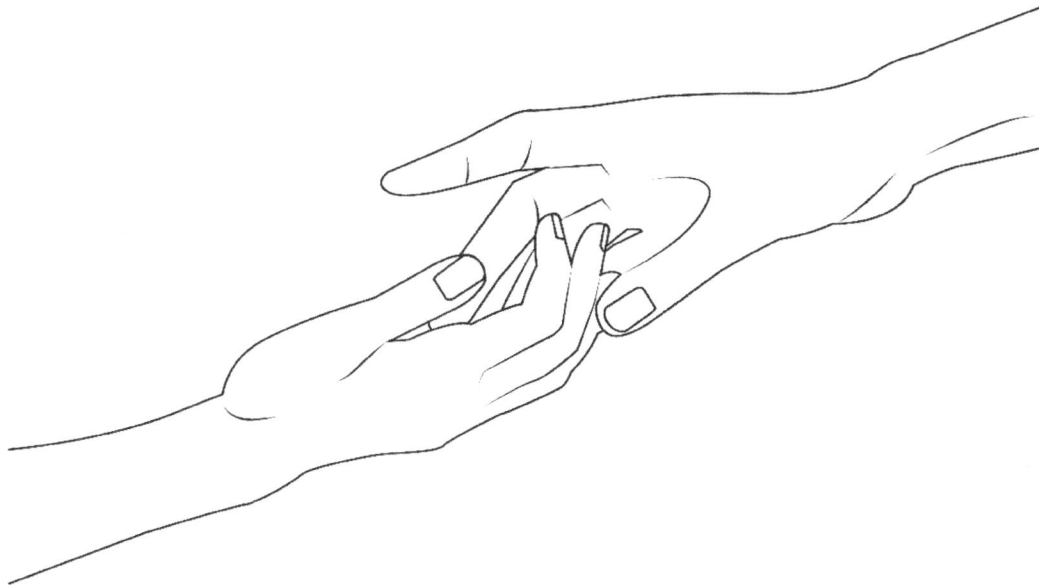

"Spiritual Formation for the Christian basically refers to the Spirit-driven process of forming the inner world of the human self in such a way that it becomes like the inner being of Christ himself."

—DALLAS WILLARD

Embracing My Inner Passion

I was awakened by the gentle sound of a voice speaking a whispered phrase that was undeniably distinct:

"Be transformed."

Barely conscious, with my eyes still shut, these audible words grabbed my attention, rousing me from a sound night's sleep. I pondered them, wondering what they might mean. Such a still, small voice, calm, but also carrying such weight!

Within mere seconds I heard the identical words spoken a second time, a little louder, with more urgency:

"Be transformed!"

Stunned, my eyelids flew wide open. Alone in my room, I wondered why this was happening. It had to be the voice of God, but why was He repeating this simple yet powerful message so emphatically?

A feeling of bewilderment swept over me. This unexpected visitation at the beginning of my day was alarming!

I was now fully awake.

A third time, louder still, the words,

"Be transformed!" rang through my ears.

I sprang to a seated position in bed. Confused and annoyed, I barked back, **"What do You want!?"**

It felt a little strange to be snapping at God, but it also seemed like He was yelling at me.

All was silent as I collected my thoughts. Then, as though I knew just what to do, I reached for my Bible. The phrase "Be transformed" was familiar enough. I knew I could find it in Romans chapter 12. I had studied and memorized passages of the Bible for years. But on this day, God had my attention. I was fully engaged. I read the following words:

> *Therefore, I urge you, brothers and sisters, in view of God's mercy, to offer your bodies as a living sacrifice, holy and pleasing to God—this is your true and proper worship. Do not conform to the pattern of this world, but **be transformed by the renewing of your mind**. Then you will be able to test and approve what God's will is—his good, pleasing and perfect will.*
> —Romans 12:1-2

For quite some time I pondered these two verses. As I leafed through the pages of my Bible, I longed for greater clarity and wisdom. My initial search revealed nothing more. My mind and heart kept returning to the very simple phrase, *"Be transformed by the renewing of your mind."* The first part, *"Be transformed,"* seemed fairly clear. God was calling me to some kind of positive change. But the phrase *"by the renewing of your mind"* both intrigued and puzzled me.

I began a simple dialogue with God. *"What do You want to say to me through this passage of Scripture?"* I asked. *"How will I be transformed?"* I asked with both trepidation and excitement.

I waited for the answer.

After several minutes of pondering and praying, I slowly began to discern that God wanted to heal my mind in some way, to renew it. Early on, painful life experiences and childhood trauma had dealt me a strong blow. I began to discern that this healing, or renewing of my mind, would somehow reprogram the negative messages continuously playing in my mind. God wanted to set me free from being defined by the anguish that resulted from a traumatic, non-nurturing, neglectful childhood. Neither of my fathers nor my mother, who suffered from her own trauma, were equipped to nurture or love a child unconditionally.

I instinctively knew healing my past memories and the shame-based thinking that shaped my soul would be a process. The negative thoughts I held about myself were deeply entrenched. A lifetime of mental repetition of negative messages had ravaged my mind.

It was humbling that God would speak to me so directly and dramatically. I was convinced that God meant it for my utmost good. Apprehension melted away. I wanted to learn more, and I was eager to begin!

Tears of joy and hope streamed down my face. Realizing the significance of this sacred moment, I made a vow to God. I wrote these words in my journal: *"Whatever it takes, no matter how long, I will dedicate the rest of my life to this effort toward transformation. Because You have so specifically chosen me for this and have made Your desire so clear, and because I know it will be for my good, I will do whatever You ask."*

It was exciting to think about what might lie ahead for me. God was calling me, and the call had beautifully and unmistakably pierced my heart and soul.

I was all in.

Discerning Your Deepest Desires

What do you desire from God? Like a garden that depends on the sun, good soil, and water to produce healthy flowers, fruits, and vegetables, our souls need to be nourished and well-maintained. What does your soul need? Do you long for more intimacy with God? In our current culture, political polarization or fast-paced living can leave us stressed, bewildered, and feeling powerless. Some people find that the worries, cares, and responsibilities of life seem to bury them in a hopeless heap of anxiety and exhaustion. Perhaps painful memories of abuse, rejection, or neglect from the past continue to haunt you. Maybe you live in a world full of people but feel alone in a crowd. You might be going through a season where you feel rejected, abandoned, or maligned, leaving you numb or in despair. Whatever the reason, you may need more of God's felt presence in your life. He cares and longs for you to invite Him in. Pause and ask God to help you become attuned to the deepest cry of your heart. Then listen for His response. Discern your most pressing desires and ask Him to meet you there.

Spiritual Practice: Journaling- "Ask, Listen, Journal, Surrender, Wait"

Take a moment to ask God to help you understand what it is you need from Him. Write out your prayer in your journal. It might sound something like this: *"Father God, please show me what my heart most longs for from You."*

- Listen for the still small voice of God to speak to your heart.

- Then formulate a one-sentence prayer describing the one or two things you would like God to do for you.- Would you like Him to help you become more aware of His presence daily or to become a more whole person?

- Do you need His healing touch, the peace of God that passes all understanding, or more of His felt love?

  - Whatever it may be, write out your request in your journal.

  - Next, pause a moment to listen for God's answer. As you continue to seek God with your whole heart, listen in the silence for the words He might whisper to you.

  - Finally, reaffirm your attitude of surrender to Him. Watch what He does, over time, in response to your prayer.

We Are All Being Formed

Whether we know it or not, every day each of us is being formed. The questions are, what are we allowing to form us, and who are we becoming? Our current culture, the things we read, and the people we spend time with all have a huge influence on the way we think, feel, and become. That's why God reminds us to guard our hearts: *"Above all else, guard your heart, for everything you do flows from it"* (Proverbs 4:23).

God wants to spiritually transform us to be more like Him in the ways we think, live, and love others. So, what exactly is spiritual formation?

Robert Mulholland describes it as "a process of being formed in the image of Christ for the sake of others."[2]

We invite God to initiate and guide the process by giving Him access to our heart. We surrender to Love. Our part is to cooperate with the work He is doing in us by drawing close to Him. The change starts from within as God renews our thoughts and perspectives and aligns them with Kingdom truths. When we learn to think more from God's perspective, we will begin to act and love more like Him and through Him. The result is a life of greater fulfillment, joy, and inner peace. It takes intention on our part.

As we learn to trust God, we become able to show up with an open, willing heart. God walks beside us as our guide and companion, every step of the way. He offers strength for the challenges and treacherous parts of the journey. He gives us encouraging glimpses of Himself along the path. He invites us into His rest, and He refreshes and revives our souls when difficulties threaten our forward movement.

He makes me lie down in green pastures, he leads me beside quiet waters, he refreshes my soul.
—Psalm 23:2-3

I've found that movement forward often requires stopping, resting, and listening to God in the silence to receive further guidance and sustenance from His loving hand. I've experienced this as a time of snuggling into the loving heart of God to gain greater understanding of who He really is. In doing so, I come to know and understand His heart and intentions for me more clearly.

Be still and know that I am God.
—Psalm 46:10

Answering Your Own Personal Call

Pause for a moment.

Imagine knowing you are completely and enthusiastically loved by the God of this universe, delighted in and cherished every minute of every day. If you could embrace that truth, how might it change your life and your ability to be at home with yourself—to be comfortable in your own skin? He can be a comfort you can depend on, even as the world seems to spin out of control and the stresses of life seem endless.

What if you knew you were never alone? When pressures like work, family obligations, or personal goals press in on all sides, what if there was a balm for your weary, distracted soul and a friend to help ease the load?

Pause again for a moment.

Close your eyes.

- Imagine a God who has your back, even on your worst days.
- Can you envision walking through life in such a close relationship with God that even in the darkest moments, His love and companionship bring joy and encouragement to your heart?
- Do you long for that kind of intimacy? Imagine God calling you to a life of wholeness, healing, and oneness with Him.
- Does any of this resonate with you? If so, how will you answer Him?
- What do you need from Him? Listen to His gentle voice asking, *"What is it that you want or need from me? I am here. I am knocking at the door of your heart. Will you open that door and share your deepest desires with me?"*

What are you sensing God saying to you today? Perhaps there is an invitation for you. If so, write your heart's answer to Him in your journal. Are you all in for a grand adventure? Write your heart's answer to that call, even if it's not completely clear what that call might mean for you at this time.

The Goals Of Spiritual Transformation

One of the primary goals of spiritual transformation is a life lived in true intimacy and harmony with a God who is good, who desires to bless us with good gifts, and has designed us for a specific purpose. Most importantly, He wants to give us *Himself*. At the heart of this union with God, the beauty of His love changes us. The more we actually experience God's loving presence, the more easily we can let go of the fear, doubt, and shame that burden our souls and hold us back.

This happened for me as I learned to simply sit quietly in His presence meditating on either a character quality of Jesus/God, a painting, or a phrase or verse found in Scripture. I would hold the picture or the words I felt drawn to during my quiet time. I repeated the words or looked at the picture several times, closed my eyes, and held the memory of them in my heart for as long as I could; absorbing the meaning or the aspect of His personhood I was sensing as important to me at that time.

A second goal of spiritual transformation is becoming more and more like Jesus in the way we love and live on planet Earth. God changes us from the inside out and forms us in His image. Each of us, in our own unique ways, take on more and more of Jesus' character. In the Greek this is called "imago Dei," or image of God. The apostle Paul casts an encouraging vision for this process in 2 Corinthians 3:18 when he says, *"And we all, who with unveiled faces contemplate the Lord's glory, are being transformed into his image with ever-increasing glory, which comes from the Lord, who is the Spirit."* This journey toward wholeness and spiritual transformation is a process that takes a lifetime. But don't let that discourage you: All the while He walks beside us offering wisdom and courage, each step of the way.

Trust And Surrender

The **heart** of the spiritual journey, meaning the core focus, is an invitation to surrender to an intimate love relationship with God. We intentionally come into His presence, receiving His healing unconditional love. We learn to trust and walk with Him in our daily lives in a continual process of surrendering. Learning to trust God is a prerequisite for surrender. This trust-walk has a positive effect on our relationships with others, our outlook on life, and our interactions with the world around us. The more we learn to trust God's loving nature, the more we will begin to treat others with love and respect. The more intimately and experientially we know God, the easier it is to trust Him.

But how does this happen, you may be asking? For me, personally, as I spent time with God, reading and meditating on His Word, the Bible, I began to see who God and Jesus really were. As I read stories about Jesus, specifically, I grew to understand His character. Then by sitting in silence in His (Jesus'/God's) presence, I began to meditate on and absorb that truth. It permeated my mind and illuminated my thinking. My love for God grew. My understanding of how He loved me began to blossom, as well. *"Do not conform to the pattern of this world, but be transformed by the renewing of your mind. Then you will be able to test and approve what God's will is—His good and perfect will"* (Romans 12:2). The changes in me were slow and subtle at first. Over time, as I *repeated* this practice of reading specific sections of the Bible I felt drawn to, the changes became more deeply grounded in truth and more easily lived out. Our renewed mind gives birth to new thoughts. And out of that, new emotions and actions are birthed. We learn to give and feel love more easily and become a more loving person. As we get to know God intimately, through His Word, we also learn to trust Him. Then surrender comes more easily. We are comfortable sharing our pain, our doubt, and our needs without shame or condemnation. This took several years. However, God met me in some pretty graphic ways through visions or visitations. These absolutely helped me along in this process by providing encouragement. You'll hear more about these visitations in the chapters that follow. I revisited (repeated) my meditative experiences several times each, in order to firmly plant the truths God revealed more deeply in my mind and heart.

Without repetition there is no transformation.

Counting The Cost

Before beginning any new endeavor, it's important to count the cost. What will it require of you? How should you prepare? What are the benefits to you? Whether it's a weight loss program, planning for a big vacation in Europe, building a dream home, or training to run a marathon, you will need to take stock and consider where you are currently, what you want to achieve, and how you will get there. What will it take to get in tip-top shape? What kinds of clothes, food, exercise, shopping, saving (money), and collaborating will best support your goals? Is there specific attire you will need to purchase? Do you want an accountability partner?

The invitation to the journey toward spiritual transformation is for everyone, but not everyone will be willing to answer the call. Why do you think that might be so?

Spiritual transformation requires many things of us.

- It involves cultivating the desire to seek and know God more intimately.
- It requires letting go of things in our lives that hold us back—like addictions, negative images of God and of ourselves, and unforgiveness.
- It involves allowing God to heal both our past and current wounds on a continual basis.
- And it requires surrender.

I often share with people that attend workshops or other events I am leading, that this intentional trust-walk, which requires surrender, usually begins with an "experiential knowledge" of God's love. I've found that most people know about God, but few have a day-to-day, moment-by-moment, experience with Him. Jesus offers us an intimate friendship, yet to many people He is a distant and unapproachable entity. As a spiritual director, I have the honor and privilege of walking alongside people who are seeking a closer relationship with God and who need to learn to experience His love personally and intimately. Part of the cost of spiritual growth involves our ongoing effort to put our trust in God, coupled with making space for God to do His work in us. I enjoyed the many times I have been present as someone experiences the thrill of hearing from God and being affirmed in His love for them.

The Healing Power Of God's Word

In the beginning there was much I didn't understand about this spiritual growth journey. I was a busy career-oriented mom with two elementary school-age children. Fortunately, we were able to enroll them in the school where I was teaching. The year was 1991. One thing was apparent: God intended to use the truth of His Word to heal the negative messages and harmful labels from my past. Going forward my path seemed to offer me an invitation to bathe my mind and heart in healing Scripture passages. This intentional focus began to transform my negative images into positive images based on how God saw me and who He uniquely created me to be. Over the next 30 years I grew in my ability to connect intimately with God in prayer and in hearing His voice more clearly.

I experienced something similar to the excitement of a child on Christmas morning who has just received a brightly-colored gift to unwrap. I spent extended periods of time each day before work reading and meditating on Bible passages. I especially focused on verses that either named me in affirming ways or that described positive characteristics of God. These focused times became a deep source of nourishment for my soul. I craved time alone with God to read, journal, and listen for His wisdom. Hearing God's voice seemed to come naturally to me. I listened for a gentle thought running through my mind that sounded like it might be God, like something that I might read in the Bible or that might be congruent with His character. I received that truth as God's whisper to me. Then I wrote it in my journal. I continued writing as I heard more of God's whispers. A journal response from and to God might look something like this:

God's whisper:

"I love you, Beverly, with an everlasting love. My love never runs out. It is constant and always available, even when you doubt me or yourself. Even when others fail you, I am waiting to hold you and soothe the ache in your heart. Get used to me loving you all the time, even on your worst days—especially on your worst days! Receive My love."

My response:

"Thank you! I receive Your love. I am humbled that You choose to love me especially on my most difficult days and through life's hardest challenges. I choose to fold into Your loving arms and drink deeply of Your peace. Please heal me and help me resist the voices inside me that compete with Your true voice."

These times of listening and responding enlivened my relationship with God. I remember emerging from my quiet room one morning. My husband, ElRoy, asked, "What do you do in that room? I finished my quiet time a half hour ago. I read the Bible and prayed, and it was good. But you seem to spend so much more time than I ever do. And you come out of that room beaming, like you've just had the best time ever! What are you doing in there?"

I paused for a moment and asked, "Do you journal?"

"No," he responded.

"Well," I began to explain, "I'm doing the same things you're doing, but I also journal using an interactive, two-way conversation with God. First, I read a passage from the Bible. Then I try to discern what God might be saying to me. Almost always, He affirms His love for me and the truths He hopes I will internalize and integrate into my life. Then I respond to Him in my journal. In so doing, I'm cultivating intimacy through an open, honest conversation with Him that is both life-giving and energizing."

This phase of my journey lasted several years, but I didn't mind. I experienced great enjoyment in the process of getting to know myself and God in new and truer ways. Old negative images of myself began fading away as new images took root in my mind and heart. Past labels like "defective" and "unlovable" were replaced with "complete in Him" and "beloved." My daily times with God were energizing and transformative. Each morning before work I dedicated about an hour to reading the Bible, meditating on key verses, and praying the prayer of my heart: *"God, heal me."* In the depths of my being, I was beginning to feel grounded in His love and in the understanding of who I was from His point of view. Over time, even on difficult days God's love seemed to wrap around me like a warm blanket. I was able to be myself more completely and sense His presence easily. I gained a deeper understanding of God's faithfulness and His desire to heal my emotions. I continued this practice, noticing gradual progress over the next ten years. I began to trust Him more deeply. This was a slow but rewarding process.

To Journal Or Not To Journal

Journaling is not for everyone. I have met many who simply don't like to journal. You may prefer to talk to God quietly and prayerfully in your heart, or share with a friend. Some may choose to simply write a phrase or a brief sentence or two in your journal, summarizing your thoughts and insights. Others may decide to process verbally with a spiritual director. Artistic expression can also be an excellent way of processing. Draw or paint your emotions. Dance or create a song of worship as an outpouring of your soul in response to what you are learning. The choice is yours. The important thing is to mentally process and reflect on what you are hearing and experiencing. Examine your thoughts and feelings regarding your communication with God. As Socrates once said, "The unexamined life is not worth living."

Get to know yourself and how you process and learn from your experiences. Be honest with yourself. Learn to do what's most effective for your own spiritual growth. Journaling is one of the ways we slow down, make sense of, and work through what God is doing in our lives. For me, it's been important to document my experiences, my wonderings, and my conversations with God so I can revisit them later. They have been a source of encouragement throughout my journey.

Spending quality time with God involves listening to our hearts as questions arise within us and sharing them with Him. Journaling became a primary tool for reflecting on my questions and wonderings, as well as sharing my needs and areas of confusion. It was easy and natural for me to fill a page or two each day with whatever was on my mind or whatever I sensed God saying. However you choose to do it, in a journal or through another method, the processing piece is essential on the journey toward transformation. It's one of the ways we allow the things we learn to go from our head (head knowledge) to our hearts (heart or experiential knowing).

Heart-knowing is what actually changes us.

Below are a few questions that might help you process thoughts and concerns related to what you've read so far. It isn't necessary to answer all of them. Select the ones that seem the most important to you.

Questions to Ponder, Discuss, or Journal

(Answer the questions that seem most important to you.)

- What are some ways you are already intentional in drawing closer to God? In other words, what tools or practices that help you grow more spiritually mature do you already incorporate into your life?
- What are some things in your life that are forming you in negative ways?
- How could you include more life-giving influences in your everyday life?
- Have you ever sensed God calling you to a deeper walk with Him?
- Are there childhood wounds or life experiences that seem to hold you back from experiencing the freedom you desire?
- What does God seem to be stirring in your heart as you think about the concepts in this chapter?

_____

_____

_____

_____

_____

Spiritual Practice: Devotional Reading

You may be thinking, *"Oh, no! Not another devotional!! I have dozens of those already."* I understand that concern. What I'm referring to here is something different: reading Scripture in a new way.

All along my path toward healing and wholeness, reading God's Word has had a profound effect on my thinking, perspective, and the daily condition of my heart. Scripture passages were food for my soul, offering wisdom, encouragement, and knowledge of God's true character.

When I read passages from the Bible that seemed to have a specific connection to my life, I read them slowly several times. I invite you to try this practice. Pause briefly after each reading to soak in the presence of God. Reading slowly and thoughtfully will allow the meaning of the words to sink deeper into your heart and your subconscious mind. In essence, it will allow the concepts to become more and more a part of your being. As you read, ask God to speak to you about how His Word can help shape your soul and your perspective. Let your heart sink deeply into God's loving presence as you silently meditate on key words or phrases that seem to carry weight and have importance for you.

Allow God's Word to bring refreshment and inspiration to your soul. This practice is called devotional reading. It is usually done using Scripture, but it can also be done using a passage from a book. The goal of this kind of reading or listening to Scripture is to "grow a relationship with God, rather than just gathering information about Him. It requires an open, reflective, listening posture."[3]

Use the texts below to practice devotional reading.

1. Look in the section below for a passage of Scripture that seems to speak to you or carry weight (importance) as you read it.
2. Read the passage three or four times, pausing between each reading.
3. Listen for God's voice or prompting.
4. Journal or jot down any important thoughts.
5. Enter into a time of rest in His loving embrace.

Scripture Passages To Read, Meditate On, Or Memorize

And we, who with unveiled faces all reflect the Lord's glory, are being transformed into his likeness with ever increasing glory, which comes from the Lord, who is the Spirit.
—2 Corinthians 3:18

Therefore, I urge you, brothers and sisters, in view of God's mercy, to offer your bodies as a living sacrifice, holy and pleasing to God—this is your true and proper worship. Do not conform to the pattern of this world, but be transformed by the renewing of your mind. Then you will be able to test and approve what God's will is—His good, pleasing and perfect will.
—Romans 12:1-2

You kissed my heart with forgiveness, in spite of all I've done. You've healed me inside and out from every disease. You've rescued me from hell and saved my life. You've crowned me with love and mercy. You satisfy my every desire with good things. You've supercharged my life so that I soar again like a flying eagle in the sky!
--Psalm 103:3-5, TPT

"Are you tired: Worn out? Burned out on religion? Come to me. Get away with me and you'll recover your life. I'll show you how to take a real rest. Walk with me and work with me—watch how I do it. Learn the unforced rhythm of grace. I won't lay anything heavy or ill-fitting on you. Keep company with me and you'll learn how to live freely and lightly."
Matthew 11:28-30, MSG

Extending The Learning

- Review and reflect on key concepts in the chapter.
- Engage two or more times in the spiritual practice of devotional reading.
- Notice the ways you are intentional this week in your process of spiritual formation.
- Ask God to create a desire in you for more of Him.
- Memorize one of the Scripture verses or passages from this lesson.

Nuggets For The Journey

You are invited to enjoy two offerings: a verse of Scripture and a prayer to begin your journey. May they be an encouragement to your soul.

Finally, brothers and sisters, whatever is true, whatever is noble, whatever is right, whatever is pure, whatever is lovely, whatever is admirable—if anything is excellent or praiseworthy—think about such things.
—Philippians 4:8

Your joy in life will depend, to a large extent, on the quality of your thoughts.

Prayer To Begin Your Journey

Heavenly Father,
You are calling me to Yourself;
to know you more intimately,
to learn how to simply "be" in Your presence, and to
understand that these times of enjoying Your presence are what I need.

Father, God, in this process I invite You to change me from the inside out,
   to heal the broken places,
      mend the wounds,
         and restore my soul.

Thank you, Father, for the truth of Your Word.
   May it be a lamp that lights my path.
      Through it, help me hear Your wisdom and encouragement
         every step of the way, as I learn to walk beside You. AMEN.

2 HOW SPIRITUAL TRANFORMATION HAPPENS

Surrendering To God's Transforming Work Within Us

"I have been seized by the power of a great affection."

—BRENNAN MANNING

Encountering Divine Love

As I entered the small chapel on a Tuesday morning, I was surprised to see so few attendees—maybe 20 or so, sitting in a circle of chairs. My spiritual director, Natalie, had invited me to hear a special guest speaker on the topic of spiritual formation. I was eager to hear what she had to say. Little did I know that this one gracious invitation would have such a dramatic, life-changing effect on my experience of God.

As Catherine began to speak, I was immediately drawn to her glowing, charismatic persona. She was lovely inside and out. She spoke with sincerity about her personal experiences. Her unfolding story revealed details of a brutally difficult life season and a debilitating illness, which had left her physically and emotionally pain-stricken for months. In order to garner a few moments of relief each day, she would relax in a warm, sudsy bathtub and soak while meditating on God's loving presence. During these meditative baths, she felt drawn closer and closer to the heart of God. Even in the midst of the pain, she enjoyed moments of peace, hope, and, occasionally, some relief from the pain.

Listening intently, I became more than a little jealous. At the time I was the busy mother of two very active toddlers, and I couldn't imagine ever having time for luxurious daily bubble baths. I imagined myself with a toddler wrapped around my legs, holding a tiny baby in my arms. *No way would this be possible*, I mused. Catherine's ability to develop a very personal, engaging relationship with God seemed elusive. How could I attain it?

From a deep place in my heart, I wanted the intimacy with God she was experiencing.

"How," I wondered, *"in my season of life, could I experience mental and emotional bliss by simply sitting in God's presence, even if I were surrounded by mountains of luxurious bubbles?"*

By the end of the presentation my curiosity had increased. I had worked up the courage to raise my hand and ask, "How can I, a mother of two very young children, experience this intimate love of God? I barely have time to use the bathroom without one of them knocking on the door."

With loving eyes, Catherine intently looked at me and calmly spoke these words: "What I think God would say to you is that He loves you so very much, and there is nothing more you need to do to earn that love. He loves you just the way you are."

Her words pierced my heart like an arrow. The message was simple. God's affections toward me were far deeper than I could fathom. Regardless of my question, how did she intuitively know that what I really needed to hear was that God already loved me? She had spoken more than mere words; they seemed prophetic. I was speechless. It was as though God was speaking directly to me through this beautiful woman sent by Him to me personally. I was unaware of anyone else in the room except Catherine and me. I felt an unexplainable energy flow through my body. It was as though I had awakened to God's unconditional love in a deeper way than ever before.

As I got up to leave the chapel, something miraculous immediately began to happen. My steps felt lighter. While walking down the stairs and along the sidewalk toward my car, I noticed a sense of weightlessness. In fact, my entire body seemed to float-walk about three inches above the pavement.

For the first time in my life, I knew what it actually felt like to be loved unconditionally! There was a growing sense within me of great joy coupled with an assurance of being gently held and cared for. Since my parents had not been capable of this kind of love, I cherished the unexpected gift I had been given.

Catherine's words became a reality that lingered in my heart for months. Whether I was at home with family, at work teaching a classroom of fourth graders, or shopping for groceries—wherever I was and whatever I did, this lighthearted sensation of float-walking stayed with me for almost a year. Since that day I have never doubted God's enduring love for me. Even as the physical sensation of the experience began to slowly fade, my confidence in God's unconditional love remained solid and sure.

My journey toward wholeness was deepening.

God Meets Each Of Us In Unique And Personal Ways

Catherine's story had elicited within me a desire for more of God. He had answered me with a supernatural experience and an internal knowing of His divine love. I was beyond surprised and so grateful! I had never experienced love quite like this before.

Prior to this experience, my religion had been based on doing, working, earning, and being a good person. After the experience, my faith-walk was based on delighting in a loving, intimate relationship of being with Him. I found great enjoyment in His presence experiencing His pleasure. I wanted to share this new-found friendship with others –to give it away.

God meets each of us in the way we can best receive Him. Your experiences will be different from mine. God knows exactly what each of us needs. Be on the lookout for ways God is showing up in your life. He won't let you down. Desire Him earnestly.

You will seek me and find Me when you seek Me with all your heart.
—Jeremiah 29:13

"Ask and it will be given to you; seek and you will find; knock and the door will be opened to you."
—Matthew 7:7

Ask yourself, *"Do I desire more of God's love, acceptance, wholeness, and healing?"* If the answer is yes, ask God and wait in hopeful anticipation of His answer. If the answer is no, then you may need to ask God to create a desire within you for more of Him.

For it is God who works in you, both to desire and to work for His good pleasure.
– Philippians 2:13 NASB

Another seed of understanding that was planted in my heart had to do with the way other people treated me. There was a sense that God was saying, *"Since you are my beloved and because I delight in you, I will treat you with gentleness and love.* This newly acquired revelation equipped me with the courage to set healthier boundaries in all my relationships.

Moving Toward Love

Most of us know about God, but we settle for head-knowledge only. We think that's good enough. Perhaps we attend church once in a while. We may even go so far as to serve in a ministry. However, there is a deeper, more intimate, experiential-knowing of God that's available for each of us. This awakening to Love sometimes happens in the midst of a season of suffering or great loss. It may happen when we realize there is much more to this relationship with God than we have previously experienced. We say yes to intimacy when we choose to move closer to God, rather than numbing the pain or filling the emptiness with distractions and imitations of God's love. The groundwork for wholeness is being laid. A gardener who tenderly cares for a grove of young fruit trees in order to enhance the fruit's flavor, prunes, waters, and watches over the trees. Likewise, we look for ways to allow God to nurture, heal, and strengthen our bruised and wounded souls so our lives bear the luscious fruit of a more beautifully healed heart.

Learning To Just "Be"

During one of my quiet times, I came upon this passage of Scripture:

> *"Come to me, all you who are weary and burdened, and I will give you rest…you will find rest for your souls. For my yoke is easy and my burden is light."*
> —Matthew 11:28-30

As someone who had very much embodied a "human doing" as opposed to a "human being," I was addicted to the affirmation that came along with my accomplishments. Yet, Jesus was asking me to simply come. Full stop! This was another specific invitation that would forever change my life. I didn't fully understand the concept of just "being" with Jesus, without having to earn His favor. The idea was foreign to me. I thought, *"Are You kidding? That's it? It's way too simple!"* But for a "human doing" with an earning-based mentality, it was more difficult to implement than I could have imagined. Still, I gradually came to embrace God's offer of freedom and fulfillment in simply *resting in His presence.* He seemed to be saying, *"Just come to Me, and My peace will be like a pillow on which to rest your weary head and calm your anxious thoughts."*

As my concept of God continued to be healed, I was able to simply be with Him authentically, in my brokenness, with honest questions. I felt more comfortable in my own skin. I was being healed of the shame-based thinking I had developed while living in a toxic family environment. I delighted in His goodness and mercy as He redeemed the dark unwanted places within me.

How Does Spiritual Formation Happen?

The Who, What, and How of Spiritual Formation

When I first became a Christ follower, I thought that the Christian life was a matter of being good, reading the Bible and doing what it said, serving in the church, and giving until it hurt. It was a demanding kind of endeavor characterized by "earning." I felt I needed to measure up to some God-ordained standard. It was a rules-based religion with very little that seemed life-giving. Over the years, my thoughts and ideas have changed quite a bit.

I didn't know there was more to desire of God until my spiritual director introduced me to a completely different way of experiencing God. I was surprised by the difference it made in my spiritual life. Once I came to understand how much God valued me as a person and wanted to just "be" with me, His invitation was irresistible. *"Come to me and I will give you rest,"* He continued to encourage me. *"I'm not asking you to 'do' anything except learn to 'be' with me and walk with me."* Slowly, my religion of earning was being replaced with a personal relationship of friendship and intimacy with Him. As I practiced walking and talking with Jesus and meditating on His Word, other things began to change. He wanted to transform my thought patterns by renewing my mind. In one of my quiet-times I was drawn to Philippians 4:8, where Paul admonished his friends to think about and focus on all that is *"true...noble... right...pure...lovely... admirable."* He seemed to be saying, *"See me in and through all of the events and conversations in your life. I am what is true, noble, right, pure, and lovely. Stay close to me and your life will be filled with more of these things."*

I believe this invitation is the same for everyone. God wants to embrace all of us and give us more and more of Himself. He desires to be with us just as we are: no masks, no hiding, and no pretending.

Have you ever experienced a time when you sensed the sweet presence of God? It may have been while watching a sunset sky change from blue to bright yellow, orange, and red, then turn to purples and pinks. Maybe it was in a warm, encouraging conversation with a friend, or a personal greeting card from someone who loves you. Perhaps it was looking into the soft innocent face of a newborn baby. It doesn't have to be a major event; it can be as small as noticing the beauty of a rose blooming in the cool of the day or listening to the waves crash of waves on a sandy shore. Try to remember a time when your heart and mind were touched by a sense of the Divine, then journal about it here.

_____

_____

_____

_____

_____

My times of devotional reading and prayer began to take on a deeper, more interactive quality. I enjoyed them so much I began to get up earlier so I could increase my time with Jesus. On weekends I sometimes spent up to two hours just reading His Word and delighting in our fellowship together. The lively conversational journal entries continued to be one of my favorite ways of communicating with Him. His presence with me felt real—palpable.

I began to experience greater joy and fulfillment as I grew to know Him in fuller and truer ways. God was leading the process. He was showing me how to lean into His love and walk alongside Him. Gradually, God began to show me things about myself. I learned that I was loved and treasured. But I also learned more about areas of pain that He wanted to heal. It became clear that my journey toward wholeness was going to require something more of me. He was inviting me to surrender to His love more completely and to embrace the path ahead as He revealed it to me. But first, He wanted me to simply pursue knowing that I was in safe hands and that I had nothing to fear.

I learned a simple practice that helped me pray easily whenever I needed or wanted to sense His presence, when my heart longed for peace or freedom from fear and anxiety. Sometimes the burden I felt for a loved one was too great to bear alone. Breath Prayer gave me a tool for drawing closer to God and allowing Him to meet my needs any time of the day.

Spiritual Practice: Breath Prayer

Breath Prayer is traced back to the desert fathers in the sixth century. It became popular in the Christian church in the East during the 14th and 19th centuries.

The word "Spirit" is "ruach" in Hebrew, and it has three meanings: wind, breath, and Spirit. So, we pray, with the rhythm of our breath, the prayer the Spirit lays on our hearts. This practice supports the idea of *"praying without ceasing"* (1 Thessalonians 5:17, ESV).

The best-known Breath Prayer comes right out of the Bible from Luke 18:13 and is called the Jesus Prayer. A tax collector prays, *"God, have mercy on me, a sinner."* But it is often shortened to, *"Jesus, have mercy on me,"* or *"God, have mercy."*

This prayer arises from our souls and is based on either a specific need or a heart full of praise. Since we are all unique and the Spirit prays within each of us, it seems appropriate that we might all have a special, individual response to our hearts' longing toward God. This short one-line prayer comes from a deep place inside of us. As we pray, we cry out for what we most desire in that moment. Below are the steps for using the Breath Prayer.

How To Pray Using Breath Prayer

1. Sit comfortably. (You can also walk as you use this prayer.)
2. Breathe slowly and rhythmically.
3. Let go of anxious, busy thoughts by refocusing your mind on the present moment.
4. Optional: Read or meditate on a short passage of Scripture two or three times to remind you that God is present with you. This will help you center your thoughts and get to a deeper place in your heart.

Example: *"Be still, and know that I am God"* (Psalm 46:10, RSV).

5. Determine a name for God that feels suitable or comfortable for you such as: God, Father, Jesus, Holy One, Kind Shepherd, etc.

6. Next, imagine God calling out to you by name and asking, *"What do you want?"* In the stillness of this moment, search your heart for an answer to this question. Some possible answers might be: *"Please give me peace." "Please, heal my son." "Provide for my family."*

7. Now, put the name for God you've chosen together with the prayer that's on your heart, like this:

Breathing in: ***"Jesus,"*** (Use your favorite name for God.)

Breathing out: ***"Please comfort my daughter."***

8. This prayer should only be about six to nine syllables. This is important because the entire prayer should fit into one in and out breath cycle.

The entire prayer should be approximately six to eight syllables long. You can be a little flexible with the number of syllables, but it's best to keep your prayer short so it fits your natural rhythm of breathing.

Breathing in: ***"Holy Father,"***

Breathing out: ***"Please give me peace."***

Breathing in: ***"Dear Jesus,"***

Breathing out: ***"Give me wisdom."***

9. Work with this prayer until it feels comfortable. Some of the words may change. That's okay. Adjust the prayer until it seems to resonate with your soul.

10. Repeat the short, simple prayer over and over again for three to five minutes. I like to use this prayer when I'm out walking alone. If there is a burden I'm carrying, it usually becomes less intense, lighter, and more manageable as I continue praying.

As the prayer flows freely and unforced, you may experience more peace and greater trust in God.

I encourage you to revisit and continue using this prayer any time of the day or night as the need arises. You may find that your prayer begins to change and get more specific over time. Allow God's Spirit to guide you in the process.

Examples of Breath Prayers:

Father, let me feel your love.

Show me your way, O Lord.

Gracious Father, heal me.

Holy Wisdom, guide me.

Let me know your peace, O God.

Jesus, please comfort me.

Lord, carry this burden.

Abba, I am your child.

Reflections On The Practice

After spending a few minutes in prayer, reflect on the process. Did your prayer feel comfortable? Did it get at the real desire of your heart? Was it short enough to fit in the rhythm of one in-and-out breath?

_____

_____

_____

_____

Sometimes while I'm walking and praying, my prayer changes slightly. Let the prayer morph into whatever you need it to be. God hears you either way, but you may feel more understood if your prayer is focused specifically on what your heart truly desires. For example, it might change from *"Dear God, please heal me"* to *"Jesus, heal my broken heart."*

Use this same prayer for multiple days, or develop a new prayer to meet the specific needs of each new day.

More About How Spiritual Formation Happens

There are four main areas of focus as we engage more fully with God in the process of Spiritual Transformation. We'll reflect on each area individually, but all four areas are interrelated, and will be explained more thoroughly in the following chapters.

Focus Area #1: Knowledge Of God And Self

Growing in the knowledge of God and the knowledge of self happens simultaneously. As we get to know God more fully, we also get to know how He views us. In other words, we get to know what is most real and true about ourselves as we get to know how God talks about us in His Word. Many spiritual philosophers and thinkers have agreed on the importance of this concept of knowing both God and self. For example, Thomas Merton noted that "There is only one problem on which all my existence and happiness depend: To discover myself in discovering God. If I find Him, I will find myself, and if I find my true self, I will find Him." Similarly, John Calvin wrote, "Without knowledge of self, there is no knowledge of God."

There are many ways we get to know both God and ourselves. Focus areas 2, 3, and 4 are some examples.

Focus Area #2: Wisdom Literature

Reading God's Word, the Bible, is the primary means of getting to know God and ourselves. The Bible contains words and stories from the life of Jesus, and it speaks from many different perspectives about God and the ways He has been active over hundreds of years. Additional writings, some historical and some spiritual, have been handed down, some from the distant past and some more recent. These writings hold truths that give us understanding into the life and character of God and His Son, Jesus, as well as insights into how we grow and mature as the people of God. Some examples of these writings include *The Weight of Glory* by C.S. Lewis, *Waiting on God* and *Abide in Christ: Daily in His Presence* by Andrew Murray, *Life Together* and *The Cost of Discipleship* by Dietrich Bonhoeffer, *True Christianity* by Charles G. Finney, *Revelations of Divine Love* by Julian of Norwich, *Practicing the Presence of God* by Brother Lawrence, and *The Pursuit of God* by A.W. Tozer. The variety of sources of ancient wisdom is almost limitless. I challenge you to choose one of the suggested books above or discover one you're more drawn to reading.

Focus Area #3: Life Experiences, Including Relationships And Suffering

We learn a lot about ourselves by paying attention to what happens in and through everyday life experiences. When we consider what is most life-giving, what brings peace and joy into our lives, and what increases our feeling of being loved, we gain an understanding of who we are. On the other hand, looking at what depletes our energy, makes us angry or sad, or what irritates us can give us clues about where we might need to focus our attention in order to cultivate a greater degree of happiness or a greater sense of closeness to God and others. Leaning into God in times of suffering can help strengthen our faith. Paying attention to our difficult relationships and what happens as we engage with others can give us clues about how to grow in our faith walk. Suffering, though not the most desirable way to grow, if we can learn to lean on God and the work He is doing in the process.

Focus Area #4: Spiritual Practices

Sometimes called disciplines or spiritual exercises, spiritual practices help us make space in our lives for God to do the work that only He can do. They help us slow down, reflect, and notice God's movements so we can lean into Him as a way of cooperating in the process of transformation. Throughout this book I'll provide a sampling of practices I found most helpful in my own formation process. There are many activities that could be considered spiritual practices. Whatever the practice is, it should lead you to come into the presence of God with the desire to get to know Him and yourself more fully, and to allow the Holy Spirit to form you.

We are not in control of the process. However, we participate in the process as we encounter God in the above four areas. God, through the Holy Spirit, does the forming. Embrace the mystery, the timing, and the way God works to complete the process of forming us into His likeness.

In my own experience, there were two important prerequisites for being able to partner with God.

The first was having a level of trust in Him. The second was embracing my own belovedness and experiencing God's love personally. I once spoke with a woman who was taking our *Heart of the Journey* class. I was stunned to hear that this missionary woman, though she served with a good heart, had never really felt God's love. We met after class and then began meeting for spiritual direction. Watching her grow in experiencing God's love was amazing. She had been a missionary for several years, working with the children of missionaries. During our class discussion, she raised her hand and said, "I have worked for God all these years, but I don't believe I have ever really known that God unconditionally loves me." She had been serving out of a sense of duty. If there is one concept, one gift I could impart to those who seek God and a life of wholeness and healing, it would be the knowledge that God deeply and energetically loves and delights in you, just as you are. It all begins here.

Questions To Ponder, Discuss, Or Journal

- Are you living with the absolute assurance of God's unconditional love? If so, how would you describe this beautiful relationship with Him?
- Consider the four areas of focus: knowledge of God and self, wisdom literature, life experiences (including relationships and suffering), and spiritual practices. Reflect on which of these areas you are most comfortable or familiar with. Then determine which of the four areas you'd like to become more familiar with.
- Have you sensed a desire for greater intimacy with God? Talk to God or journal a prayer to Him about your desire.
- How has God met you in a very personal way? Describe what that experience was like?

_____

_____

_____

_____

_____

Scripture Passages To Read, Meditate On, Or Memorize

Select one or more of these Scripture references to read and ponder. You might want to read the whole chapter the verse was taken from to get a fuller understanding of what God wants to speak to you.

He is the one we proclaim, admonishing and teaching everyone with all wisdom, so that we may present everyone fully mature in Christ.
—Colossians 1:28

...we will remain strong and always sincere in our love as we express the truth. All our direction and ministries will flow from Christ and lead us deeper into Him, the anointed Head of His body, the church.
—Ephesians 4:15, TPT

He predestined [us] to be conformed to the likeness of His Son...
—Romans 8:29, TPT

May the Lord answer you when you are in distress; may the name of the God of Jacob protect you. May He send you help from the sanctuary and grant you support from Zion. May He remember all your sacrifices and accept your burnt offerings. May He give you the desire of your heart and make all your plans succeed.
—Psalm 20:1-4

As the deer pants for streams of water, so my soul pants for you, O my God. My soul thirsts for God, for the living God. When can I go and meet with God?
—Psalm 42:1-2

Two Spiritual Practices: Slowing And Noticing

These two practices work well together. **Slowing** is one way to overcome addictions to inner and outer hurry, busyness, and workaholism. Through slowing, the sacrament of the present moment is tasted to the full. We learn to savor each moment.

In order to practice slowing, we can try being deliberate in using a few of the following strategies:

- Intentionally drive in the slow lane.
- Get plenty of sleep. Take a nap when you need one.
- Speak more slowly.
- Look people in the eye when you're in a conversation.
- Chew slowly and thoroughly. (It's also great for your digestion.)

- Sit longer at the table, enjoying the food and the company.
- Plan buffer time between meetings or appointments so you can relax and regroup.
- Intentionally stop working through your breaks at work.
- Take time to breathe slowly.

Over time, engaging in slowing will help us grow in patience (the ability to wait with grace), receive interruptions graciously, trust in God's unhurried schedule, and keep company with Jesus as we live at a more relaxed pace.

Noticing involves paying attention to our lives and the activity of God in everyday experiences, such as a visit with a friend, helping someone in need, taking a walk in nature, or listening to worship music. Intentionally noticing where and how God shows up is a huge part of growing spiritually. After all, we cannot cooperate with God's movement if we do not notice how He's present with us and what He's doing in us.

As you practice noticing, try to tune into the following elements as you experience them.

Moods	Cloud patterns	Wind patterns
Sights	Attitudes	Relationships
Sounds	Thoughts	Activities
Smells	Feelings	Spiritual experiences
Tastes	Sensations	What is life-giving
Textures	Hopes and dreams	What is life-draining

Spiritual Practice: Noticing

1. Stop at any time of the day to intentionally notice God and His activity.
2. Notice what you hear, see, smell, etc. (Use the chart above.)
3. Ask yourself one or more of these questions:
   - When have I sensed God's presence today?
   - When have I felt joy today?
   - When did I feel loved or appreciated today?
   - What sights, sounds, smells, tastes, or textures captured my attention today?
   - Where did I experience the strongest feelings today? Why or how?
   - What relationship was a blessing for me today and why?
   - What was most life-giving today?
4. Quietly meditate on the answer to one or more of the questions.

5. Journal about what you are thinking, feeling, desiring and noticing as you reflect on one or more of the questions.

Both of these practices are relatively easy to do. Try intentionally *practicing slowing* and *noticing several times this week.*

The practices become effective when repeated over time.

Reflecting On The Practice (Journal Your Answers Below.)

·   Which of the above practices (slowing and noticing) were you most drawn to, and why? If you didn't enjoy or enter into the practices, what was the reason?

·   Was there a time of the day when you were more able to focus on the practices? Morning? Evening? Weekends?

·   Sometimes we talk in terms of *resistance*, which is when we turn away from something because we'd rather not do it. Did you sense any *resistance* as you engaged with the practices of slowing and noticing? Why might that have been?

_____

_____

_____

_____

_____

Extending The Learning

·   Take time to do each practice in this lesson (breath prayer, slowing, noticing) a couple of times.

·   Memorize or meditate on a verse or passage of Scripture you felt most drawn to.

·   When or how did you experience God's love for you this week?

·   Journal the ways God has shown up for you this week.

·   What one or two concepts from this chapter seem important for your spiritual growth?

Nuggets For The Journey

Reflect on the prayer below by Catherine of Siena. Enjoy her descriptions of God.

You, O eternal Trinity, are a deep sea,

into which the more I enter the more I find,

and the more I find the more I seek...

O eternal Godhead what more could you give me

than yourself? You are the fire that ever burns

without being consumed;

you consume in your heat all the soul's self-love;

you are the fire which takes away cold;

with your light you illuminate me so that

I may know all your truth.

—Catherine of Siena, as cited in the Lion Book of Famous Prayers[4]

3 GETTING TO KNOW GOD, PART 1

Our Distorted Images Of God

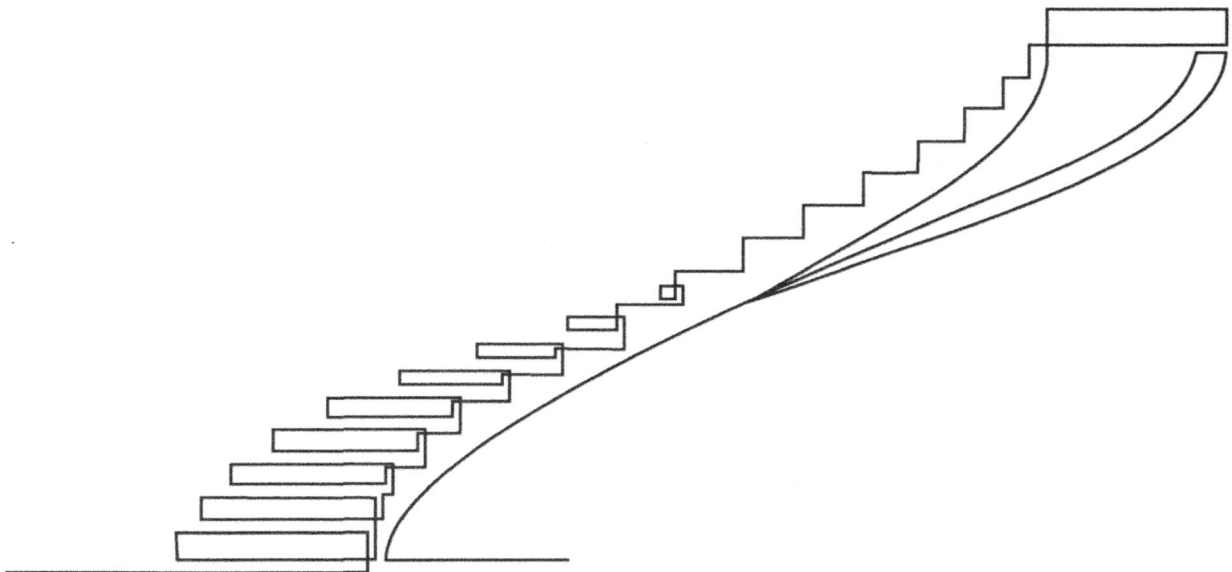

"All human troubles come from thinking about God wrongly."

—DALLAS WILLARD

The Lost Safety Pin

"Can I have a baby sister?" my five-year-old self asked my mother longingly. "We'll see what we can do about that," she replied vaguely. Having tea parties on the upstairs balcony with only my porcelain doll felt lonely. Finally, when I was six and a half, my wish came true when my baby sister was born.

Mom often called upon me to help in small ways. On one occasion, as I watched her change my sister's diaper, one of the safety pins broke. Exasperated, she commanded me, "Go get me another large safety pin from the junk drawer." Obediently, I ran to the kitchen and opened the drawer. It was brimming with disorganized odds and ends. I frantically began moving things from side to side. "Hurry up, I need that pin," my mother's impatient voice rang from the back bedroom. I searched intently, but to no avail. "Did you find it? I need it now!" The intensity in her voice was increasing. I feared her anger. Panic-stricken, I struggled to look harder as my anxiety rose. All this effort was accomplishing nothing. Gripped with fear and frustration, I yelled, "I can't find it!"

Even the thought of my mother's imminent disapproval felt threatening. She rushed into the kitchen with a diaper hastily wrapped around my sister's bottom. Like a woman on a mission, she reached into the drawer, and briskly slid a few items out of the way. She picked up the safety pin and snapped, "IT WAS RIGHT THERE! COULDN'T YOU SEE IT?" I stood frozen in stunned silence. How could I explain my incompetence? She had expected much more from me. Seeds of self-doubt and shame were taking root in my soul. What was wrong with me that I couldn't find the pin? Despite my best efforts, I was not enough. At the time I couldn't fully describe my feelings. I simply knew I had failed miserably.

Scenes similar to this one occurred often. My mother's disapproving look and tone undermined my self-esteem. I endured her outbursts, never balanced by intermittent times of affection, encouragement, or approval. I don't remember ever feeling the warmth of her arms wrapped around me or the soft kiss of her lips on my cheek. She didn't or couldn't express physical affection. If she had, it may have softened the blow of her angry tone and words. It could have lessened the intensity of the disapproval I felt from her but, alas, there were no hugs.

One of my mother's pet sayings was, "It wasn't from the thorns she died. It was from the lack of roses." Then she would pause and just stare at me. As a young child, it was confusing and overwhelming to hear her talk like this and not understand why. I knew, by the look on her face, that she was disappointed with me; that something had to be my fault, but she never explained. It seemed like a coded message, a negative indictment of me as a person. I was too ashamed and afraid to ask questions.

I felt quite alone in this painful, shame-filled place. I never knew when the next explosion would be unleashed upon me. Over the years I grew to believe that I must be defective. Though I tried to be as good as I could in order to live up to her expectations, it never seemed enough.

My mother always tried to provide for my physical needs. Though we had very little, there was always food on the table. Sometimes it was only gravy bread, a single piece of white bread smothered with a tasteless brown gravy, which was hard for me to stomach.

We always had hand-made Halloween costumes. She also made my school dresses, one for each day of the week—although she let me know that she had to go without buying bras so she could afford material for my school clothes. I felt ashamed at the knowledge that she was going without so I could have what I needed. Though many of my physical needs were met, she was not able to offer emotional support. That, I would have to learn to provide for myself. I didn't understand it then, but looking back, it seems that mom had an underlying anger that she carried with her always. Over time, I developed a habit of playing alone and shying away from people. It just felt safer.

The Stairwell Beating

Early one morning a clash of hostile voices erupted in another room of the house. I ran to see what was wrong just in time to catch a glimpse of my mother running from her bedroom. She headed toward the staircase of our upstairs duplex, which led to the front door. Her blood-curdling scream shot fear through me as she shouted, "You get away from me!" My father followed closely behind her and caught up halfway down the staircase. My grandparents on my dad's side happened to be staying with us at the time. They stood beside me at the top of the stairs holding onto me as I watched helplessly. My father brutally beat his fist into my mother's head. Crouched down on one of the steps, she sobbed as she tried to fend off his vicious attack. I noticed the large ring on my dad's finger, which he was using to intensify the blows. Streams of blood began to trickle down her face.

I can still almost hear my grandmother pleading with my grandfather, "Dewey, do something!" As a small-for-my-age ten-year-old, I knew I was no match for my father. I began crying uncontrollably. My grandfather, a quiet, reserved man, tried to talk my dad into stopping, but he continued with his savage beating. Finally, when my father had done enough damage to satisfy his rage, he fled through the front door without a word. Noticing my swollen eyes and trembling body, my grandmother said, "We can't send her to school like this."

Later that day, I learned that my mom had locked the door and called the police, to request a restraining order. It would be many years before I would see my father again, but the trauma of this and other violent, physical outbursts of his temper stayed with me into adulthood. Alcoholism, anger, and emotional instability had plagued my father and brought chaos and fear to our family and to me personally.

Reflecting On The Story

One way we learn to understand what God is like and whether we can trust Him is by how we were treated by our primary caregivers. Other authority figures such as teachers, pastors, aunts and uncles, bosses, and others can also affect how we imagine God to be. What I learned from being raised by emotionally unhealthy parents was that:

1. Authority figures may not be safe or trustworthy.

2. Love is conditional and must be earned.

3. Shame is debilitating, and causes us to hide.

As you read the two stories in this chapter, did you relate to the pain of not feeling safe or cared for emotionally? You may be aware of your own childhood struggles, which may have resulted in negative images of God. All of us grow up with some negative images of God. For the most part, these distorted images have their roots in childhood trauma. Repeated traumatic childhood interactions with unhealthy parents can affect how we live out our lives and relationships with others. The good news is that emotional healing is possible. With intention and consistent effort, God can redeem what was stolen from us in childhood. I will share more on that topic as we move through the chapters of this book.

I began my faith walk with God in my early teens, hopeful that He could fill the void I felt in my life. I had already learned to toe the line and follow the rules. Fear is a great motivator, so it was easy for me to commit to living out the basic principles of the Bible. I wanted God's approval and longed to feel close to Him. However, my relationship with Him was centered on obedience, duty, and obligation to a demanding authority figure. My sense of salvation was based on being good, and most importantly, on not making God mad. I had heard that God could fill the deep void in the center of my being. That void had left me lonely and aching for love, but something seemed to be in the way of me experiencing God without all the strings attached.

Out Of The Frying Pan, Into The Fire

My mother filed for divorce after 12 years of marriage. She promised me she would never marry again. I was relieved, but you know what they say about "the best laid plans of mice and men." In under a year she introduced me to a man she had been dating. They had met at a dance club and were secretly married not long after. He was hot-blooded, domineering, and emotionally abusive. It soon became obvious that he resented Mom having kids from a previous marriage; there were three of us by then. Upon returning home from school, I would sometimes find his handwritten notes by the phone commanding me to fulfill tasks: "Fold the laundry!" "Clean your room!" These notes were often signed in oversized capital letters, **"GOD!"** My fear-based view of authority figures had gained additional negative support.

As I grew up, I continued to be serious about my faith. My commitment to God was steadfast. I faithfully went to church, read my Bible, and helped teach children's Sunday School classes. I noticed a discrepancy between how I felt about God compared with the loving God of church sermons and the hero of Bible stories. To me God seemed distant, a little demanding, and punitive. Did this far-away God know and understand what I was going through? Would He find time to reach down and rescue me from the painful life I was living? I wondered if He even noticed me. Did He really care? What would it take to measure up, to earn love and help from a God who seemed distant and probably busy with more pressing issues?

I sometimes prayed, *"God, where are you? Why have you left me alone in my pain and misery? I want to believe you care, but sometimes I don't know if you are really there. If there is no help, then there is no hope of ever living free from the fear and affliction of my situation. I wanted to run away, but where would I go? Please help me!"*

In my agony, I related to the author of Lamentations, who wrote:

> *Because of the LORD'S great love we are not consumed, for His compassions never fail. They are new every morning; great is your faithfulness. I say to myself, "The LORD is my portion; therefore, I will wait for him."*

The LORD is good to those whose hope is in Him, to the one who seeks Him; it is good to wait quietly for the salvation of the LORD. It is good for a man to bear the yoke while he is young...

For no one is cast off by the LORD forever. Though He brings grief, He will show compassion, so great is His unfailing love. For He does not willingly afflict or grieve anyone."
—Lamentations 3:22-33

I could not see a light at the end of the tunnel. I felt that without God's intervention I had no hope. I longed to one day to know God as more than I had experienced up to that point in my life. I chose to wait on Him, but not very patiently.

Who Is God, Really?

Every one of us carries a mental picture of God. We think of this as our concept of God. But this is not only an image we hold in our minds. Actually, along with what we have been taught to think about God, our *experiences*, our *memories*, and our *feelings* also play a large part in forming this total picture. The most important part of how we live out our spiritual lives is based on our "felt-ness" of who God is. What we feel He is really like can determine our openness to God and our ability to receive His love.

A surprising number of genuine Christians are caught in an inner conflict between what they have been taught about God and how they think He feels toward them. For example, we may have heard or been taught that God is loving and kind, but what we really feel about Him is that He is distant, aloof, and a harsh task-master. Or, we may have been told that God is our provider, but our difficulty paying the rent some months causes us to doubt it and to feel He is uninterested in our plight.

Growing up in an unhealthy family system further emphasized the distance between what I'd been taught about God, what I felt, and how I experienced Him. How do we get to the bottom of what is most true about God? How do we discern the difference between the image of God we carry in our hearts, what we know intellectually, or are taught about God? The following quote by Paul Steeves gives us a clue:

Our real idea of God may be buried beneath our conventional prayers, conventional worship, and conventional doctrines. To dig down to these real notions and to replace them with the correct ones will require an intelligent and vigorous search and perhaps painful self-examination.[5]

As you continue reading this book, you will be introduced to tools and exercises you can use to help with this deep-dive search for truth. I can vouch for the fact that this "vigorous search" is worth your time and effort. Your freedom and wholeness may depend on it. Living in alignment with the truth of who God is, rather than believing a lie, is definitely a priceless gift God is waiting to give you.

Reflections on the Stories

1. What thoughts or emotions came up as you read my stories?

2. Were you able to get in touch with your own experiences that have affected your image of God or your ideas of how God sees you? If so, journal below.

3. Does the vigorous search for who God truly is seem like an exciting adventure or a daunting task?

4. Are you ready to begin? If not, what do you need to do to get ready?

_____

_____

_____

_____

_____

Two Spiritual Practices: Confession And Self-Examination

There are two spiritual practices that, working together, help us as we go through our rigorous search for truth about ourselves and God: Self-Examination and Confession.

Adele Calhoun describes **Self-Examination** as a "process whereby the Holy Spirit opens my heart to what is true about me. This is not the same thing as a neurotic shame-inducing inventory. Instead, it is a way of opening myself to God within the safety of divine love so I can authentically seek transformation."[6]

Confession "embraces Christ's gift of forgiveness and restoration while setting us on the path to renewal and change."[7]

When used in the context of this chapter dealing with our distorted images of God, these two practices can enable us to look at what is false about what we believe and feel about God and why that might be.

Note: *If using the word Jesus instead of God is helpful or more pleasing to you, feel free to do so. For some,* *the word "God" carries a negative connotation or feeling, usually based on past painful experiences with a mother or father figure. Use the name for God that presently causes you the least amount of distraction.*

Activities To Ponder, Discuss, Or Journal

I have created three activities to help you explore the origins of your false images of God. You can do all of them, or simply choose the ones that seem to apply to your situation. I suggest that if you do all three, you take a break in between each one to reflect or to allow your mind and heart to rest. It will be most helpful to do these activities when you feel curious and ready to do the work, not rushed. Each activity will focus on a different aspect of understanding your image of God. Each one falls under the main category or spiritual practice of confession and Self-Examination. The practices of reflection and journaling are also included in the activities. Before you begin, you might want to spend some time in prayer asking God to continue His work of healing and restoring your soul. Healing of past painful experiences takes time. It's nice to know that God is patient and will walk through this season of restoration of your soul with you. You may also want to enlist the support of a friend, counselor, or spiritual director as you journey through this process.

Activity 1 - Current Negative/Abusive Experiences And Their Effects

Directions: Listen to your heart. Are there *current* negative experiences or relationships with key people in your life, nagging disturbances to your sense of well-being or peace of mind? Some people to consider include your mother, father, siblings, grandparents, aunts, uncles, teachers, bosses, religious leaders, and friends. The idea is NOT to focus on all of these relationships, just the ones that seem especially troublesome. List those people and negative experiences. Then describe any feelings that come up for you. **Take your time as you discern which people and negative experiences might be helpful for you to unpack at this time.**

Current difficult Relationship with Related Feelings	Current negative Experience with Related Feelings	Current Earthquake Events with Related Feelings

Activity 2 – Past Events And Relationships That Have Negatively Affected Your Image Of God

Directions: On the chart below or in your journal, list any *past* events or relationships that may have negatively affected your image of or relationship with God. Especially consider what I call *earthquake events*, such as war, death, major sickness, accidents, handicaps, physical or sexual abuse, loss, betrayal, etc. Describe the negative event, difficult relationship, and related feelings you experienced. Then describe how negative feelings from that event or relationship may have carried over into your thoughts and impressions of God and your relationship with Him today.

<u>Past</u> Negative Events with Related Feelings	<u>Past</u> Difficult Relationships with Related Feelings	Earthquake Events with Related Feelings

Activity 3 – Negative Character Traits Of God/Jesus

Directions: Review the list below and *circle the negative character traits* that seem or feel true for you regarding God/Jesus. In other words, you may have head knowledge telling you that God is supposed to be kind and caring, but in actuality, you feel that He is detached, too busy, or distracted with more important things. This activity helps us zero in on who we feel God is.

Circle The Negative Traits About God You Feel Are True.

Unconcerned	Controlling
Cold	Distant
Far away	Mean
Too Busy	Abusive
Detached	Hard Taskmaster
Bothered	Unjust
Disinterested	Harsh
Demanding	Above it all
Critical	Absent
Judgmental	Tough
Unapproachable	Preoccupied
Uncaring	Angry
Rigid	Abandoning

Killjoy Absent	Distracted

Reflect on the negative aspects of God's/Jesus' character you circled and that you may feel are unpleasant or uncomfortable. Why does this seem true for you? Are there any particular traits that stand out?

Journal a response to God regarding your reflection. Perhaps you might let Him know how you feel and ask Him to show you what is true about God. You could ask Him to show you a Scripture to meditate on that speaks in an encouraging way about this feeling. There are several examples of Scripture later in this chapter. Pause a moment and reflect on the verse below then journal a response to God.

Yet the LORD longs to be gracious to you; He rises to show you compassion. For the LORD is a God of justice. Blessed are all who wait for Him!
—Isaiah 30:18

_____

_____

_____

_____

_____

Activity 4 - Positive Character Traits Of God/Jesus

As you discover your felt image of God and compare it to what is true about who He really is, more healing can take place.

Directions: Review the lists below and *circle the positive characteristics of God/Jesus* you would like to experience more of in your life. The results of this activity can be a starting point in discovering how God may want to reveal Himself to you.

Caring	Tender
Affirming	Nurturing
Generous	Giving
Interested	Welcoming
Near	Accepting
Listening Intently	Loving
Holy	Calm
Life-giving	Involved
Concerned	Connected

Passionate	Unconditional Love
Reliable	Friendly
Kind	Ama Mother
Trustworthy	Abba Father
Happy	Provider

Reflect on the positive aspects of God's/Jesus' character that you find **hard to embrace**. Why do you think this might be true for you?

_____

_____

_____

_____

Journal your answer to this question. Talk to God about your feelings and thoughts and ask Him to show you more of His true self. Ask Him to specifically show you how He displays His character traits in your life, or where joy and peace are present in your day.

_____

_____

_____

_____

Years ago, when I completed this activity myself, it became clear how unhealthy traits of my parents and negative childhood experiences were reflected in my felt image of God.

> *Our operative God image is often a subtle combination of our mom and our dad or any other significant authority figures. Once we begin an inner life of prayer and in-depth study of sacred texts, we slowly begin to grow and move beyond childhood conditioning. From then on it only gets better. Grace does its work and creates a unique "work of art." Much religion is merely early conditioning, and not yet God experience for oneself.*
> *—Richard Rohr, "Creating God in Our Own Image"[8]*

This may seem like a lot of work, but uncovering the source of our negative image(s) of God is a very important factor in the healing process. It can lead us to discover truer images of God that will allow us to embrace His love and live in freedom out of our true selves.

Scripture Passages To Read, Meditate On, Or Memorize

I recently reread a verse found in Philippians. Paul describes how little everything in this world means to him when compared to the indescribable joy of knowing God. Of course, he was referring to a very intimate, personal knowing of God. Select one or more of these verses to meditate on this week. Which ones ring true for you? Why or why not?

> *I consider everything a loss because of the surpassing worth of knowing Christ Jesus my Lord, for whose sake I have lost all things. I consider them rubbish that I may gain Christ.*
> *—Philippians 3:8*

> *He tends his flock like a shepherd; He gathers the lambs in his arms and carries them close to His heart; He gently leads those that have young.*
> *—Isaiah 40:11*

> *Yet the LORD longs to be gracious to you; therefore He will rise up to show you compassion. For the LORD is a God of justice. Blessed are all who wait for Him!*
> *—Isaiah 30:18*

Extending The Learning

Take a few moments at the end of each day this week to reflect upon the following three questions from the traditional prayer practice called the *prayer of examen*:

1. When/where/how did I sense the love or presence of God in my life today?
2. When/where/how did I **not** experience the love of God, or when was I **not** sure of His love in my life today?
3. How can I lean more fully into God's love and presence tomorrow?

Let your daily prayers reflect the desire of your heart to be *healed*, to be *whole*, and to be *restored*.

_____

_____

_____

_____

_____

Nuggets For The Journey

In the next chapter, "Getting to Know God, Part 2: Embracing God's True Character," we'll explore how we come to know and experience God's true nature in the depths of our being. We were created for fellowship with God and others. In fact, intimate relationships are one of the most fulfilling aspects of life. God is waiting with arms flung wide open to receive you and to allow you to get to know Him, as you are fully known by Him.

4 GETTING TO KNOW GOD, PART 2

Embracing God's True Character

"You have made us for yourself, O Lord, and our hearts are restless until it rests in you."

—ST. AUGUSTINE

A Surprising Encounter

Our destination was Italy: country of romance, home of ancient Roman ruins, rolling hillsides covered in bright golden sunflowers, and, at every restaurant, pasta smothered in delicate savory sauces followed by the best cappuccino in the world! Around every corner was a unique photo opportunity and a different flavor of rich, creamy gelato to try. My favorite combo was chocolate with pistachio.

While on pilgrimage to significant spiritual sites throughout Italy, our first stop was St. Peter's Basilica in Rome. Built in the ornate Renaissance style, it showcases gigantic works of art surrounded by marble columns, stained-glass windows and doors, and a roof lined with over a hundred life-size marble statues. There was something sacred about the basilica's artistic and architectural beauty that made me stand and gaze in awe.

A deep yearning for the presence of God was drawing me. Years ago, on my first-ever trip to Rome, I had visited the basilica on three separate occasions over a ten day period. I simply could not get enough of the sense of holiness and the majestic presence of God I found there. My favorite work of art was *La Pietà,* a marble sculpture created by Michelangelo.

As we approached St. Peter's Basilica, my heart beat faster, excitement piquing. I could hardly wait to get inside. I knew exactly what I wanted to see. As I walked through the doorway, my eyes rose to see the beautiful dome overhead, also created by Michelangelo. Considered the tallest dome in the world, every inch contained brightly colored marble mosaics trimmed with gold.

I separated from my group. Alone, I made my way toward Michelangelo's *Pietà,* one of his most loved sculptures, the only one he ever signed. My love affair with this work of art consumed me. I was mesmerized by what the artist had done with one large solid, off-white piece of marble. Mary, the adoring mother, held across her lap the wilted body of her crucified Son.

My eyes were drawn to Mary's gentle face, so serene and kind but also filled with grief. I focused intently, gazing into her winsome face, pondering the beauty of her welcoming expression. She seemed lifelike enough to talk to. As if I were being swaddled in a warm blanket, I was held in the silence by a Presence that seemed to draw me closer. My heart was filled with an assurance of God's love in this most intimate moment.

I was aware that the love Mary expressed for her beloved Son was quite different from the detached, non-nurturing relationship I'd experienced with my own mother. Still, as I waited, savoring this moment, I sensed God's healing touch caressing the loss, depravity, and brokenness of my childhood.

Then, I sensed a subtle internal prompting to ask Mary a question. I knew it was my heavenly Father I was talking to when I whispered, *"Will you be my mother?"* A strange thing to ask, I thought, but I had followed the prompting. As I did, gentle, healing tears began streaming down my cheeks, as I waited for Her answer. I knew that what I was really asking was for God to fill the void inside of me, left there because of the absence of a nurturing mother's love. Within me grew a deep and experiential-knowing of God's gentle kindness. I felt tenderly held in His arms as the more feminine, nurturing qualities of God seemed to encircle me and penetrate my entire being. As I allowed His Spirit to deeply immerse my soul, a visitation of God's comforting love swept over me like a refreshing breeze.

As a mother comforts her child, so will I comfort you...
—Isaiah 66:13a

I continued silently praying that God would meet me in my desire to be loved and held by Him. Over the next few moments as tears continued to stream down my cheeks, I felt swept up into a state of being affectionately surrounded by Pure Love. I absorbed as much healing presence as I could hold. This image of a gentle mother's arms, holding her Son, represented the same loving arms that held me close. In that moment love was the truest thing about me. I was deeply loved.

Can a mother forget the baby at her breast and have no compassion on the child she has borne? Though she may forget, I will not forget you! See, I have engraved you on the palms of my hands.
—Isaiah 49:16a

This penetrating experience would live long and vividly in my memory as I continued to ponder and gain a greater understanding of the breadth and depth of God's gift. Michelangelo's stunning marble image would forever be a tangible reminder of holy, compassionate love.

I was awakened from this almost trance-like state by a gentle touch on the shoulder. It was time to go. I had spent the entire time allotted in front of this one heavenly statue—time well spent and well worth the price of admission.

Reflections On The Story

G.K. Chesterton once wrote, "Let your religion be less of a theory and more of a love affair."[9]

I allowed myself to continue engaging in this love affair with God. This experiential knowing of God's love seemed to be a growing theme in my life. It was part of a deepening journey into the heart of God. The heart and soul of this journey was learning to be in an intimate love relationship with the One who loved me and whose love could heal the broken places.

What was modeled to me in childhood was a very conditional love, one based on my fulfilling the role of a perfect daughter and sometimes even a caretaker to my own mother. There had never been enough of me to attain this place of perfection. But God, in His wonderful mercy and grace, was offering me a different kind of love—a love freely and lavishly given. All I had to do was reach out and receive it.

Intimacy Involves Slowing Down

Early in my spiritual formation journey, Jesus invited me to slow down and make time for intimate connection with Him. This became a discipline, or a practice, I tried to incorporate into my daily life. It wasn't easy, but I was determined. Whenever possible, I intentionally simplified my schedule by eliminating activities that added stress or pressure. I learned to stop seeing myself as a "Yes" person who would jump in whenever anything needed to be done. Over time I learned to say nicely but confidently, "No." I also incorporated a slower approach to reading my Bible. I read slowly, meditating on its truth. I lingered over verses and passages that God's Spirit drew me to, like magnets to my soul. Sometimes the lingering, over just one Scripture, lasted for several days. I would spend my entire morning quiet time focusing on one passage of Scripture: reading, rereading, pondering, meditating on, and journaling back and forth to God on that one passage of Scripture. His Word became a part of my heart and soul, as I was drawn closer and more deeply in love with a God who wanted to reveal himself to me, and whose love is limitless.

We get to know God best in relationship with Him, and relationships develop when we spend time together, sharing intimate moments. David Benner, author of *The Gift of Being Yourself,* calls getting to know Jesus within the context of a relationship "transformational knowing." We are spiritually transformed as a result of our personal experiences and conversations with God.

Why don't you try it for yourself? Choose one of the Scripture passages that speaks to your heart. Read it, meditate on it, copy it in your journal, and begin a conversation with God regarding the thoughts and questions that come up for you. Then answer your question the way you think God/Jesus might answer them.

Scripture To Read, Ponder, Meditate On, Or Memorize

The intimacy of God's presence contrasted with the more forgetful love of my earthly mother is fleshed out in the verses below:

Can a mother forget the baby at her breast and have no compassion on the child she has borne? Though she may forget, I will not forget you! See, I have engraved you on the palms of my hands...
—Isaiah 49:15-16a

You have searched me, Lord, and You know me. You know when I sit and when I rise; You perceive my thoughts from afar. You discern my going out and my lying down; you are familiar with all my ways. Before a word is on my tongue you, Lord, know it completely. You hem me in behind and before, and You lay Your hand upon me. Such knowledge is too wonderful for me, too lofty for me to attain. Where can I go from Your Spirit? Where can I flee from Your presence? If I go up to the heavens, You are there; if I make my bed in the depths, You are there. If I rise on the wings of the dawn, if I settle on the far side of the sea, even there Your hand will guide me, Your right hand will hold me fast.

If I say, "Surely the darkness will hide me and the light become night around me," even the darkness will not be dark to You; the night will shine like the day, for darkness is as light to You. For You created my inmost being; You knit me together in my mother's womb. I praise You because I am fearfully and wonderfully made; Your works are wonderful, and I know that full well.
—Psalm 139:1-14, NIV UK

As a mother comforts her child, so will I comfort you...
—Isaiah 66:13a

Intimacy In Prayer

As I was able to receive more of God's lavish love, I also learned that He wanted to know me personally, and embrace all of me, even the broken parts. He was inviting me to share the pain I had endured living with parents who were unable to nurture me as a child. He wanted to nurture my wounded soul. This knowledge became the focus of many of my times of prayer. I learned to be open and authentically myself with Him. I began to talk to Him about the things that held me back and kept me stuck. He could handle all of it. He already knew. There was no need to hide. In those days my journal entries were my prayers. It was easy and not uncommon for me to spend between an hour and a half or two hours in Bible reading, prayer, and journaling during my morning quiet times. I couldn't get enough of God's love letters to me through His Word.

My journal entries were two-way conversations with God about what I had just read or what I was experiencing and feeling. The presence of God was palpable, like a bit of heaven had opened up all around me. I could almost touch the essence of God. After writing a thought, or a question, or even a paragraph to God, I would pause in the stillness and listen for His response. I was new at this, but almost without fail, I would sense God's response to me. I trusted that these encouraging words were from Him. I wrote them as I seemed to hear them in my mind.

All the while I was getting to know His character. Stories in the Gospels told me about the life and character of Jesus, God's only Son. Other passages affirmed these truths and revealed even more about the character of God and His Son. Even though I'd been a Christ follower for at least 20 years and had read and studied the Bible, this was different. I savored the sweetness of our fellowship and the depth of our friendship.

I love the book *The Shack*, which was later made into a movie. If you've seen the movie or read the book, you know God the Father, His Son, and the Holy Spirit interact with the main character in the most beautifully personal, supportive ways. The conversations and activities they do together portray a priceless image of love, honesty, and respect. My quiet times were very much like that, very personal and authentic.

Prayer As "Being, Waiting, Listening, And Responding"

Sometimes we treat prayer like a series of short texts or emails. When we're in need of something we just shoot one off and trust that God is available to receive the message. We hope He has downloaded an instant alert app so He can answer immediately. As I'm racing down the freeway at top (legal, of course—*wink*) speeds, I pray, *"God, I'm running late. Please get me through this snarl of traffic—in the next two minutes would be good."* I might throw out a quick prayer of desperation, *"I need a parking place, now!"*

Prayer can be focused on asking for things, for sure; in fact, we're encouraged in the Bible that God gives good gifts to those who ask. *"Every good gift and every perfect gift is from above, coming down from the Father..."* (James 1:17a, ESV). *"If you, then, though you are evil, know how to give good gifts to your children, how much more will your Father in heaven give good gifts to those who ask Him!"* (Matthew 7:11). God is our Provider in times of need.

And God is there for us when we call out to Him. God is our Strength and our Helper in times of trouble. He is our Rock in the midst of a storm. *"From the end of the earth I call to You, I call as my heart grows faint; lead me to the Rock that is higher than I"* (Psalm 61:2).

> *O Lord, my strength and my stronghold, my refuge in the day of trouble...*
> *—Jeremiah 16:19a, RSV*

Just Being With God

There is another kind of prayer that captured my heart: just **being with** God, spending time with Jesus, gazing into his face, or simply waiting in His Presence. I needed no agenda other than to make myself available to receive whatever God had for me at the time. He sometimes chose to speak to me in the silence as I listened and focused on Him. Other times, I simply felt a sweet knowing of His Presence with me. These were beautiful, refreshing moments of being available to God. He *became the Restorer of my soul, my Comforter, and my Resting Place.* Other times I chose to give back to God by expressing praise, gratitude, and adoration for who He is and all He has done. *God was the Giver of all good gifts, my King, the One I adored.* Sometimes I sat with Him, imagining Him holding me in the midst of a painful memory or situation. During these quiet moments when I came to Him in my brokenness, restlessness, and pain, I sensed His compassion and acceptance. I received *Hope, as His Loving Presence was like ointment for my wounds.*

Prayer is an invitation to step out of the false security of our image-focused, distracted lives, which are characterized by only "head knowledge" of God. We come to Him with our uncertainty, chaos, pressures, and questions and enter into a relationship of the heart. We learn to allow His loving, healing arms to wrap tightly around us and to hold us. We allow Him to deeply know us and to show Himself to us. From this place we also get to know the many aspects of His character. We often think of God as Love, Goodness, and Kindness. However, He is also Holiness, Mystery, and Majesty. This experience of the full spectrum of God's character ushers in a transformational knowing where we are truly changed on the inside. We let God, in all of His many qualities, into the deepest places of our heart and soul, and over time, He makes us whole.

I invite you to make time to lean more deeply into quieter, restful, tender moments with God. He wants you to wholeheartedly enjoy the safety of His being and experience the warmth of His friendship. Let God pursue you, spend quality time with you, and heal your heart and soul in the process. Ask God to make His felt presence real. Then rest in Him as you experience your own intimate moments with Him. Open your heart to the ways He chooses to reveal His healing love to you. Invite Him into a deeper conversation about what He brings up within you. You may want to ask a question or ponder how part of the story relates to you. Wonder silently or through journaling by asking, *"What part of this story applies to me? What do You want to show me about Your care and desire for me?"*

Questions To Ponder, Discuss, Or Journal

- How would you describe your prayer life today? Is it vibrant, intimate, and relational, or is it dry, lack-luster, and uninspired?
- If you could change one thing about your prayer life, what would it be?
- What do you most need from God/Jesus right now? Are your prayers and quiet moments with Him spent seeking fulfillment of that specific need from Him?
- When you pray, are you completely honest and vulnerable with God, trusting that he cares and wants to meet your needs?

_____

_____

_____

_____

_____

Scripture Passages To Read, Ponder, Meditate On, Or Memorize

He who did not spare His own son, but gave Him up for us all—how will He not also, along with Him, graciously give us all things?
—Romans 8:31-32

Who shall separate us from the love of Christ? Shall trouble or hardship or persecution or famine or nakedness or danger or sword? No, in all these things we are more than conquerors through Him who loved us. For I am convinced that neither death nor life, neither angels nor demons, neither the present, nor the future, nor any powers, neither height, nor depth, nor anything else in all creation, will be able to separate us from the love of God that is in Christ Jesus our Lord. --Romans 8:35-39

Praise the Lord, O my soul, and forget not all His benefits—who forgives all your sins and heals all your diseases, who redeems your life from the pit and crowns you with love and

compassion, who satisfies your desires with good things so that your youth is renewed like the eagles. The Lord works righteousness and justice for all the oppressed...The Lord is compassionate and gracious, slow to anger, abounding in love. He will not always accuse, nor will He harbor His anger forever; He does not treat us as our sins deserve or repay us according to our iniquities. For as high as the heavens are above the earth, so great is His love for those who fear Him; as far as the east is from the west, so far has He removed our transgressions from us. As a father has compassion on His children, so the Lord has compassion on those who fear Him.
—Psalm 103:2-13

Spiritual Practice: Visio Divina

Visio Divina sets an interior stage for a soulful connection with our Maker where intimate communion is possible. It encourages the practice of viewing all of life through a sacred lens, uncovering the messages hidden within creation and other creative works of art. All of life then becomes hallowed ground and our souls are expanded. In his book *The Universal Christ,* Richard Rohr writes, "Authentic God experience always expands your seeing and never constricts it...In God you do not include less and less; you always see and love more and more."[10]

For this practice you will need to pick a piece of art you are drawn to or even a beautiful element of nature, such as a flower or mountain peak. I have often used the art print by Rembrandt known as the *Return of the Prodigal Son.* You can find it online.

Step 1: Identify the piece of art or object that will be the subject of your reflection. Then pick a comfortable place where you will not be disturbed or distracted. Relax. Closing your eyes and focusing on your breath can be a helpful way to center yourself in the divine.

Step 2: Gaze at the entire picture. Notice the shapes, the colors, and the lighting. Notice the detail of both the foreground and background. Once you have visually canvassed the artwork, note what has drawn your attention. Just like in Lectio Divina, it is God who is inviting you to a treasure meant just for you.

Step 3: Meditate on the part of the picture that has drawn your attention. How is God speaking to you? Why do you think God drew your attention to this particular part? Is a message conveyed that pertains to your life today? Do you sense an invitation? Do you hear a call? Is a memory aroused? Allow these thoughts to descend to your heart. What emotion is evoked? What word describes your inner stirring as you embrace this feeling? Allow God's communication to touch you deep within where the Spirit dwells.

Step 4: God has been speaking to you as you meditated on this artwork. It's now time for you to respond to the Divine. Allow your words to be born in the recesses of your soul. What is your response? What is your prayer? Articulate any yearnings or desires that arise. Give voice to the emotions whirling within.

_____

_____

_____

_____

_____

Step 5: Words are never sufficient to express our deepest selves. Turn to silence to simply rest in communion with our Creator—the One who kissed your soul before placing it in your body—the One who loves you beyond measure. Savor the stillness. Be soothed by His Love.

Extending The Learning

Usually, one particular aspect of God's character attracts us. It is often an aspect of God's nature that meets our needs at a given time. For example, when I experience the passing of a close friend, God (the Holy Spirit) becomes *my comforter*. When I am lonely or afraid, God becomes my companion or my protector. When I think, "There is never enough.", God becomes my provider and sustainer.

It's important to have a balanced view of God's character, to know Him as both a loving and kind God as well as a righteous and Holy God. The more we become comfortable with experiencing God's true character with all of its many facets, the more we will become comfortable surrendering to His transformational work in us.

Who is God for you today?

_____

Nuggets For The Journey

- Revisit the spiritual practice, Lectio Divina, using a story from the Bible in which Jesus is one of the main characters.

- On several occasions I've revisited the following story by Julian of Norwich as an encouragement to surrender to God, who loved us enough to create us and to look after us. Sometimes the simplest of truths are the most profound. Open yourself to God and allow Him to nurture your soul through this beautiful little story:

> He showed me a little thing, the size of a hazelnut, in the palm of my hand, and it was as round as a ball. I looked at it with my mind's eye and I thought, "What can this be?" And the answer came, "It is all that is made." I marveled that it

could last, for I thought it might have crumbled to nothing, it was so small. And the answer came into my mind. "It lasts and ever shall because God loves it." And all things have being through the love of God.

In this little thing I saw three truths. The first is that God made it. The second is that God loves it. The third is that God looks after it.

What is He indeed that is maker and lover and keeper? I cannot find the words to tell. For until I am one with Him I can never have true rest, nor peace. I can never know it until I am held so close to Him that there is nothing in between.

—Julian of Norwich, "He Keeps All that Is Made"[11]

5 GETTING TO KNOW OURSELVES, PART 1

The False Self

"*The world breaks everyone, and afterward, some are strong at the broken places.*"

—ERNEST HEMMINGWAY

Healing An X-Shaped Wound

Early one Sunday morning, after an emotionally heated conversation with a family member, I was desperate for relief from the intensity of the conflict. I longed for a loving connection with God and for His reassuring presence. Sitting down in the comfy leather chair in my quiet time room, I began to intentionally still my mind. Leaning against the wall in front of me was a collage I had made. My eyes focused on a black and white, close-up magazine picture of a young girl's face. Her eyes were closed as she leaned on someone's chest, their hand lovingly stroking her hair. I imagined that someone to be Jesus. Frequently, this picture became the starting place for my personal time of meditation. When I thoughtfully gazed at the picture, I was usually able to relax and begin to open myself to the presence of God. I began wondering if, in my imagination, I could become the girl in the collage being lovingly embraced by God. Closing my eyes, I hoped to see myself safely leaning on Jesus' chest, His hand caressing *my* hair.

As I waited in the silence, I was surprised by what I saw. In my mind's eye, an image of myself at age ten appeared, standing alone against a stark gray cement wall. I wore a crisp white short-sleeved dress. Curly dark brown shoulder-length hair framed my face. Covering most of my body was a horrific gaping wound in the shape of an X. It extended from my shoulders to my thighs.

Startled, my eyes flew wide open. My mind was gripped with both agitation and shock. Slowly, I began making mental and emotional connections between the image of the X and my mother's negative remarks toward me during my formative years and even into adulthood. Her sharp statements could be critical and off-putting and often came from out of nowhere. They eroded my personal self-worth. The image of the X left me intrigued and puzzled, wondering what God might want me to know. I sensed there was more. Sitting in the stillness, I pondered the meaning of the vision. I was anxious to gain greater clarity. As I continued to consider this vivid vision of myself, I realized the X was a symbol of the wounding messages of worthlessness and shame from my past.

Once again, I meditated on the picture of the girl whose hair was being caressed by Jesus. When I closed my eyes a second time, that same picture of myself appeared, with the X partially covering my body. But this time, a hand, which seemed to be the hand of Jesus, entered the scene from the right side. Slowly and gently, He peeled away both sides of the X, one at a time, without causing the slightest bit of pain. Then, He carefully applied a soothing ointment to the raw wounded area where the X had been. Gradually, I began to understand that God was giving me a visual representation of His desire to heal me from the emotional wounds of my childhood.

I felt encircled by God's presence as deep within me grew an assurance that He was, indeed, performing a healing work in the vulnerable places of my soul.

Stunned by the vividness of the vision and the power of God's presence, I sat quietly, basking in the wonder of such a profound visitation, melting into His nurturing love. My sense of worthlessness began to fade as I allowed what I had seen to settle in my mind and into the broken places of my heart. I was growing in the knowledge of my own worth in the eyes of God. His gentle treatment of the wounded area further impacted my understanding of how tenderly He cared for me. I felt known and treasured.

Eventually I opened my eyes and realized I had completely lost track of time. Our church's Sunday service would begin shortly, and I didn't want to be late. Thankfully, I arrived in time for worship.

Throughout the service I continued to carry an unmistakable sense of God's presence, characterized by a lightness and a freedom to worship more fully. I entered in with confidence and uplifted hands, The residue of my experience that morning felt like a fountain of joy bubbling over. I told no one of my experience, but simply held the beautiful memory of it in my mind and heart. I was curious. Was there more?

Later that day, I couldn't get my mind off of the images I had seen earlier. Wondering if it would be possible to reenter the scene again, I returned to the burgundy leather chair hopeful that God might have even more to reveal. As I sat and closed my eyes, God's presence fell upon me as it had that morning. I waited in anticipation, hoping I wasn't being too presumptuous. I focused my full attention on God's presence within me.

Within seconds the scene replayed itself from the beginning. First, I saw the image of me as a young child branded with an X, then the hand of Jesus gently removing the X, and finally the application of the healing ointment. But this time, the vision continued. Jesus' hand appeared a second time with healing salve. Dotting the salve along the wounded area, Jesus began repeating the words *"I love you with an everlasting love. I love you with an everlasting love"* with each application, until the salve covered the entire wounded area. I sat mesmerized as a third time Jesus' hand appeared, now holding a threaded needle that He used to stitch up the X-shaped wound, one section at a time. I watched all of this in stunned amazement. In my wildest imagination, I could never have conjured this.

The scene went dark. The images vanished and a pitch blackness covered everything. There was no sign of the girl, the X, or Jesus' hand. Waiting in the silence, it wasn't long before I began to see a tiny shimmering golden object forming in the far distance. The closer it came, the more easily I began to recognize the shape of a small X made of pure gold. It came to rest alone on the blackness. Gradually in the distance there appeared a second shimmering golden shape. As that image drew closer, I could see the shape of the letter O. One by one, a series of X's and O's formed until there were four X's alternating with three O's lined up in a U shape, all resting on a table covered with a black cloth: X, O, X, O, X, O, X. I smiled. Actually, I felt like laughing out loud. It was clear to me that the ugly X-shaped wound had been exchanged for a beautiful golden necklace made of X's and O's. I recognized these as symbols of love and friendship. My former feelings of shame and worthlessness continued to diminish. In their place were feelings of acceptance and of being valued for who I was. I watched the scene come to its conclusion as Jesus, surprisingly, lifted the golden necklace and placed it around my neck.

The vision ended, but its essence continued to stir feelings of pleasure and delight. I sat in the stillness for a long while, soaking in the profound mystery and wonder of Jesus healing my woundedness. God had opened my mind, heart, and imagination to receive an amazing vision, showing me His miraculous power at work deep within me.

Reflecting On The Story

God had gotten my attention. My understanding of who I was had changed forever. He had taken my childhood messages of shame and unworthiness and replaced them with messages of value and acceptance. My mind was being renewed and transformed through a revelation of who I was from God's point of view. I had also grown in my ability to enter into His presence with ease, intentionally surrendering myself to receive His pure, extravagant love.

What were your thoughts as you read my story? Pause for a few moments and consider the following questions:

- Not everyone hears God in the same way. In what ways has God spoken to you or prompted you?
- What are some of the ways God has revealed something of Himself and His character to you? What thoughts and feelings do you experience as you revisit moments of God's revelations?
- Could you identify with my struggle with feelings of shame and worthlessness? If so, what memories or thoughts came up for you? Do you sense a desire for healing from past wounds?

_____

_____

_____

_____

_____

Pause, ponder and pray: Ask God what He might want to show you—how He may want to meet you, or speak to you through this story. Listen for His still small whisper inviting you to come closer.

Revisiting moments of God's presence or blessing can be faith-building and encouraging. I journaled the unfolding story, not wanting to forget a single moment of this visitation.

Doing The Work Involves Surrender

Accessing God's transforming work in our lives involves us partnering with Him and surrendering to His deeper work within us. We do not earn transformation by our own efforts, but our effort is needed in the process. He does the transforming as we make efforts to give Him greater access to our hearts and minds. God's transforming work in us often comes as we ask for help in a situation or with a relationship. When we ask, we are, in a sense, surrendering to His guidance and His will. Surrendering to God or trusting in Him are both prerequisites for preparing our hearts to allow Him to work more completely in us.

Personal Inventory: Getting To Know Our False Beliefs

Looking at what we actually believe about ourselves is a good starting point. Begin by noticing which statements below seem to be true for you (what you currently believe about yourself), or which statements someone has said about you. These are the kinds of statements we would never say to another, especially a friend. However, we consciously or unconsciously rehearse these in our minds, because we have heard them and have come to believe them. Check all that apply.

_____In order to be loved I must be perfect/good.

_____I'm too much trouble.

_____How stupid of me to make that mistake!

_____I'm a disappointment.

_____I'm a bottomless pit.

_____I wish I'd never been born.

_____I'm defective/bad.

_____I'm unlovable.

_____I'm unwanted.

_____What was I thinking?

_____I'm way too sensitive/emotional.

_____With a past like mine, how can God use me?

_____As a Christian I shouldn't be struggling with my weight/anger/depression/anxiety, etc.

_____Why do I cry so easily? It makes me look weak.

_____Don't be so selfish/stupid.

_____Don't rock the boat; just ignore whatever is bugging you.

_____My value is based on how much I do for others.

_____I am well-liked only when I'm doing well/agreeing with others/fun to be with.

_____My value is based on what others think about me.

_____I should be ashamed of myself.

Write your own self-defeating statements in your journal if they weren't included in the list above.

_____

_____

_____

_____

Now, take a few minutes to determine which statements above seem to carry the most emotional weight. Can you identify one or more of the strongest messages you received as a child? Do you remember who spoke them to you? Can you recall what the person actually said and in what context? Perhaps nothing was actually said out loud. It might have been a look of disdain or a gesture of rejection. It may have been an implied message, like a sigh of disapproval. Using the chart below, try to recall the event, time, place, and person who spoke or communicated the negative words or messages to you. Include as many details as you can. Recalling negative labels helps you know what needs to be addressed. This does not necessarily mean the words were/are true.

Negative Labels And Messages

Negative Statement or Gesture	Person Speaking or Implying	Context (when and how)	Your Thoughts and Feelings on the matter

False Narratives

It's easy to get caught in the trap of negative beliefs about ourselves that are based on the false narratives spoken to us by uncaring or unthinking people. Remember, "Hurt people, hurt people." Consider the source when someone casts an undeserving, negative judgment upon you. We need to get in the habit of refuting negative labels. We are not our past or our parents' past. We are not the labels that were placed upon us as children.

It takes effort and commitment to unlearn or replace the negative messages for the truth of God's Word.

If you'd like to extend this activity, consider answering this question: How do you think these negative messages may have affected your life and relationships with others, with God, or even yourself? Many people grow up feeling a kind of self-loathing based on the way they were treated as children. Some pull away from relationships, have difficulty trusting, or difficulty making decisions and commitments. Try to determine what effects false narratives have had on you. Journal your answer as you explore further thoughts and feelings.

When you're finished, write a short response from God to you, at whatever age you were at the time. Make it an encouraging statement reminding yourself of how God feels and thinks about you and how you know that to be true. You might need to go back to previous chapters to remember what you've already explored about God's character, as well as His thoughts and feelings toward you.

Your response may sound something like, *"Thank you for seeing me as your beloved daughter/son and friend. I chose to believe that I am loved just as I am. I reject the negative label and lean into your perfect love."*

Wherever you are in the process, your responses to God need to be honest. Intimacy is based on an honest, open dialogue. Be as vulnerable as you can with the One who loves you.

_____

_____

_____

_____

_____

Ways We Hide: Developing The False Self

Many of us have grown up with a negative self-image. When this happens, we sometimes use techniques to hide from what we consider the undesirable or less acceptable parts of ourselves. Hiding can cause us to avoid really knowing and accepting ourselves. We begin to develop what is often referred to as a false self. The false self is an image we build, a persona we invent based on what we think others want from us or what will be more acceptable. We may learn how to earn other's approval, but if we are hiding our true self, we will not be able to form intimate relationships. Close relationships "besties" are formed when we share our experiences, our joys, and our pain with a trusted person who listens well and allows us to be open and honest. When we begin to feel more at home with ourselves, others will relate to us more easily.

Earning Approval

I worked hard to get good grades in my high school college prep courses which, finally, gained me a few accolades from my mother. However, any kudos I got for straight A's only reinforced my belief that I was only acceptable if I was *practically perfect in every way* to quote one well-known nanny. Consequently, I grew up with a very weak sense of personal identity, I began to believe that I was good or approved of only if I accomplished something spectacular. My unmet emotional need for unconditional love precipitated my sense of not measuring up and left me feeling lonely, unloved, and defective. I continued to do well in as many areas of life as possible in order to prove my worth: a worthiness based on earning and good behavior.

Being loved is not about behavior. Anytime we are affirmed for something we do; it is not love. It is only approval. Approval is not all bad, but it can lead to our striving for it by continuing to perform, strive, and work hard; mistaking it for love.

The problem was not that I did certain things well or had competencies and abilities that helped me succeed. The problem was the inordinate investment of time, emotion, and energy I began to place in my image. The life path I was on, characterized by attaining a form of perfection and success, made me feel somewhat valued. However, I didn't intrinsically feel that I was valued as a person.

I don't remember my mother ever hugging me or telling me she loved me. Much later in life, I asked her why she was never physically or verbally affectionate. She blankly stated that she hadn't been nurtured as a child, so she didn't have the capacity to nurture me. This sad truth disturbed me at my very core. No verbal or visible signs of remorse or regret. Just – "I didn't have it to give." This left me with a knowing feeling in the pit of my stomach that stuck with me.

Hiding The True Self

Our false self can also manifest itself when we learn to cover up the parts of ourselves that seem less desirable. We may be drawn to classical music or tennis, but they're just not popular with our family or friend group. In order to be more accepted, we might pretend we like the genre of music or the sport that seems most acceptable to others. Consequently, we hide our desire for what we really prefer. Perhaps someone finds out we like light opera or pairs ice skating and makes fun of us. As children, we are vulnerable and haven't developed ways of protecting our delicate egos, so the injured parts of us go into hiding. We might even go as far as making fun of others who like tennis or light opera in order to hide our natural enjoyment of them.

Looking at the list below, check any/all of the ways you sometimes avoid unwanted feelings or thoughts. Don't be surprised if you find yourself checking most of the listed items. This personal inventory can be useful in moving us toward spiritual and emotional growth through greater self-knowledge.

The Ways We Hide Or Numb Our Thoughts And Feelings

_____**Busyness**: Our days are filled with endless to-do lists, appointments, meetings, and tasks to accomplish.

_____**Over-work**: We work overtime or go into work early, stay late, or habitually eat at our desks during lunch and break time. We may even extend our work week into the weekend.

_____**Codependence**: We often find ourselves helping someone else: helping, self-sacrificing, or caretaking at our own expense.

_____**Addictive Behaviors**: We use drugs, alcohol, shopping, eating, cleaning, TV, sex, gambling, staying busy, technology, etc. to numb our pain.

_____**Perfection**: We strive for flawless actions and/or appearance in order to achieve acceptance and love.

_____**Tyranny of the "Shoulds"**: We feel that we should meet every need that arises. We find it extremely difficult to say no.

_____**Keeping Secrets**: We keep secrets that no one else knows, not even our most intimate friends or family members. These are not terrible things we've done, just things we feel ashamed of. For example, they could be what some people call "white lies" etc.

_____**Pretending**: We act out a part or pretend so that others will have a more favorable impression of us, like pretending an off-color joke told in a social setting doesn't bother us, so we look like "one-of-the-gang."

_____**People-Pleasing**: We give, serve, and do compulsively out of a need to be recognized, noticed, appreciated or loved.

Facing and being honest about our fears, negative attitudes, past hurts, and hidden selves can be a difficult painful process. The more we accept and embrace the reality of who we are, the fears that haunt us, the shame that plagues us, and the addictions that keep us numb to our past or current reality, the sooner we can bring these areas into God's healing light. As we embrace the gentle, accepting love of God, we can learn to offer ourselves that same compassionate acceptance.

Eventually, we learn to stop avoiding difficulties and start welcoming the freedom that comes from facing and working through painful memories and experiences. We become more keenly aware that compassionately embracing and integrating these challenges leads to spiritual maturity and growth. But we can't do this alone. God is our guide and companion along the path. It may also be wise to consider enlisting the support of a safe friend, counselor, or spiritual director as we begin to face the different ways we hide, numb, or avoid unwanted or unpleasant thoughts and feelings.

Questions To Ponder, Discuss, Or Journal

1. How does the thought of living as your true self feel? Does it make you anxious or afraid? Is it too risky? Have a conversation with God about your apprehensions if you have any. What do you think God might want to say to you?

2. We are much more able to navigate this journey of healing and wholeness with the help and encouragement of others. Have you reached out to a friend for support? If

not, spend some time seeking God in prayer as you search your heart for someone who is safe and exhibits wisdom and Godliness.

_____

_____

_____

_____

_____

By His very nature, God is always with us, though we can learn to be more present with Him. Meditate on the passages below, asking for more felt awareness of His loving presence.

Scripture Passages To Read, Pray, Memorize, Or Meditate On

"...and lo, I am with you always (remaining with you perpetually—regardless of circumstance, and on every occasion), even to the end of the age."
—Matthew 28:20, AMP

You, God, are my God. Earnestly I seek you; I thirst for you, my whole being longs for you, in a dry and parched land where there is no water. I have seen you in the sanctuary and beheld your power and glory. Because your love is better than life, my lips will praise you as long as I live, and in your name, I will lift up my hands. I will be satisfied as with the richest of foods; with singing lips my mouth will praise you. On my bed I will remember you. I think of you through the watches of the night. Because you are my help, I sing in the shadow of your wings. I cling to you; your right hand upholds me.
—Psalm 63:1-8 NIVUK

Spiritual Practice: Imaginative Prayer

Imaginative Prayer is sometimes referred to as Gospel meditation. It is a prayer connection that grows out of meditating on and visualizing Gospel stories as we meet Jesus in them. We develop an authentic relationship with Jesus because we share in this experience with Him. These shared experiences bring about a deeper level of trust and comfortableness, which enables us to live out of our authentic selves. The result is often a more intimate relationship with God as we move from head-knowledge (informational) to heart-knowledge (experiential).

This practice can be done alone or in a group. When alone, you will need to silently read the prompts to yourself before each reading. In a small or large group one person reads the Scripture passage while another person reads the prompts. I have found that doing this in a group setting can be especially powerful for two reasons: the listeners are free to close their eyes and let their imaginations lead them wherever God's Spirit takes them, and participants can be invited to share their experiences. So much can be learned from this intimate sharing. However, this practice can also be effective when you are alone. Be patient with yourself as you learn to tap into your God-given imagination and enter into the Gospel story. This will become easier over time.

You will be both an observer and a participant in the story. Enter in as fully as you can. If you are unable to enter in, simply focus on the storyline, and rest in the truth of God's Word as you read or as it is being read to you.

About The Practice

- The primary goal of this practice is to meet and interact with Jesus in a Gospel story so that your experiential understanding and knowing of God can deepen.
- You or someone else will read a chosen Gospel story three or four times.
- Before each reading you will read or someone else will read a prompt describing what to look for or focus on.
- After each reading you will be given an opportunity to meditate on the story, as well as your personal response to it.
- After the third reading you will be given an opportunity to journal about your experience or conversation with Jesus. It can be helpful to play soft wordless or unfamiliar instrumental music as you journal.
- At the end of the practice the facilitator may invite you to share your experience with your small group or within the larger group.

The goal of imaginative prayer is to be present with Jesus in the story and to experience the events in the story with Him. You lean into your imagination rather than your intellect. Your focus will move from a head-knowing to a heart-knowing of Jesus. To help with this process try to imagine the story using all of your five senses: Hearing, tasting, seeing, touching, and smelling. This will bring the story more alive.

The Process

Choose a Gospel story where Jesus is involved as one of the characters. You can choose any Gospel story, but it may be more effective if you choose a familiar story, one you've been drawn to in the past. It's best to choose a relatively short story, since you will be reading it three or four times. If your story does seem longer, you might want to only read it three times. In a group setting, the facilitator will choose the story for you.

Reading #1: Read the passage to get familiar with what's happening and who the characters are. You are an observer.

Pause for about a minute to silently **ponder** the Scripture and **notice** what you see and hear.

Reading #2: Read the passage in order to get in touch with how you might experience the story using your five senses. What would you see/notice, hear, feel, smell or taste if you were right there experiencing the action and conversations in the story?

Pause to silently **ponder** the Scripture and **notice, using your five senses.**

Reading #3: Read the passage again, but this time enter in as one of the characters. Who do you see yourself as? Continue to use your five senses. Pay special attention to Jesus and how He sees you or responds to you. How does your character feel? What does the story look like from the perspective of the character you have chosen to be?

Pause, ponder, and give yourself 15 minutes or so, to journal your **noticings**.

Reading #4: Read the story again but without an agenda.

Set your journal aside and simply rest in God's loving presence when the reading is finished. Give yourself as much time as you desire.

Now, Let's Try The Practice

Find a quiet space to allow yourself the privacy to focus on God's presence with you. You may choose a passage, or use the one I suggest, the story of Jesus calming the sea, found in Mark 4:35-41, RSV.

Begin by closing your eyes and centering your attention on God's presence with you. Now, take a few slow deep breaths. Pray for guidance and inspiration.

Reading #1: Listen to (or read) the story to get a basic idea of what it is about and who the main characters are. Try to visualize what is happening in your mind's eye as you observe the characters and the conversations.

> On that day, when evening had come, He said to them, "let us go across to the other side." And leaving the crowd behind, they took Him with them in the boat, just as He was. And other boats were with Him. And a great windstorm arose, and the waves beat into the boat, so that the boat was already filling. But He was in the stern, asleep on the cushion; and they woke Him up and said to Him, "Teacher, do you not care if we perish?" And He woke up and rebuked the wind, and said to the sea, "Peace! Be still!"
>
> And then the wind ceased, and there was a great calm. He said to them, "Why are you afraid? Have you no faith?" And they were filled with great awe, and said to one another, "Who then is this, that even the wind and the sea obey Him?"

Pause, Ponder, And Notice.

Reading #2: Read (or listen to) the story a second time. Use your imagination along with your five senses. What tastes, smells, etc. are you aware of as you ride along in the boat with the waves beating against it? What sights and sounds do you see and hear? You're still an observer, but you are becoming more and more aware of what is happening around you.

Read the same Scripture passage as above. (Mark 4:35-41 or whatever Scripture you have chosen.)

Then Pause, Ponder, And Notice.

Reading #3: As you read or hear the story for the third time, enter in as one of the characters. Who do you feel drawn to be? What do you do and who do you interact with? What do you say? How do you feel? Pay special attention to Jesus. Does he look your way? If so, how would you describe the look on His face? Do you interact with each other in any way?

    Read the same Scripture as above.

Then Pause, Ponder, And Journal (10-15 Minutes).

_____

_____

_____

_____

_____

_____

_____

_____

_____

Reading #4: This time simply read or listen to the story with no prompt or agenda, other than leaning into God's loving, protective presence. Set your journal aside.

    Relax, rest, and lean into God's presence.

    Read the same Scripture as above.

    Pause and be with God.

Spend three to five minutes in silent reflection. If you're doing this in a group, share among yourselves.

Reflecting On The Practice

- How was your experience with Imaginative Prayer? What was meaningful or helpful for you? If you were not able to enter the story, why do you think that might be?
- What character in the story did you become?
- Did you experience any type of interaction with Jesus? If so, what was it like for you?
- Was there anything specific that God revealed or spoke to you?

_____

_____

_____

_____

_____

As you continue to practice Imaginative Prayer, you may hear a word or receive a prompting. Other times you might hear nothing. During those silent moments as you wait in God's presence, allow yourself to let go of expectations, and trust that God is working in you to establish love and truth deep within your soul.

Extending The Learning

Reading Bible stories in which Jesus is one of the main characters is a good way to deepen your experience of God's true character. The more times you engage with this practice the easier it becomes. Some people have a difficult time accessing their imagination. Know that your imagination is as God-given as your body and your mind. You can use your imagination to grow spiritually. Choose a different Gospel story and practice imaginative prayer as you sense God's invitation to do so.

You might try choosing a Gospel story that helps counteract an unpleasant feeling or situation, or one that affirms your belovedness.

Some examples are:

- The woman with an issue of blood: Mark 5:25-34 or Luke 8:42b-48
- The woman at the well: John 4:1-29
- The woman caught in adultery: John 8:3-11
- Jesus feeding the five thousand: Matthew 14:13-21
- The woman who washed Jesus' feet: John 12:1-8
- Jesus washing the disciple's feet: John 13:1-17

Nuggets For The Journey

Above all things and in all things, O my soul, rest always in God. For He is the
everlasting rest of the saints. Grant, most sweet and loving Jesus, that I may
seek my repose in You...For my heart cannot rest or be fully content until,
rising above all gifts and every created thing, it rests in You.
—Thomas a Kempis[12]

6 GETTING TO KNOW OURSELVES, PART 2

Embracing Our True Selves

"THERE IS ONLY ONE PROBLEM ON WHICH ALL MY EXISTENCE, MY PEACE AND HAPPINESS
DEPENDS: TO DISCOVER MYSELF IN DISCOVERING GOD. IF I FIND HIM, I WILL FIND MYSELF, AND
IF I FIND MY TRUE SELF, I WILL FIND HIM."
—THOMAS MERTON

Family Tree: Vision Of Destruction And Renewal

During one of my morning quiet times, I had been pondering the threads of pain and grief that ran through my family of origin. Multiple divorces, broken relationships, alcoholism, and untimely deaths each brought with them sadness and grief. The memories of the suffering surrounding each devastating event weighed heavily on my mind that day. It felt like an attack on my personhood meant to destroy hope, to discourage and bring me down.

As I so often did, I closed my eyes, my heart reaching out to God. In the stillness my mind landed on a familiar Breath Prayer: *"Jesus, heal me."* So simple, yet from the depths of my heart, I cried out to God. Then I continued in silence to be present to God. Within a few minutes a vision began to unfold before me.

Standing alone in a wooded area, I noticed a single tree separated from the rest. I was aware that the tree represented my biological family: my personal family tree. From the left, a stranger entered the scene. He was a rather seedy-looking character with disheveled hair and a chin covered in bristly stubble. He was a typical cartoon-like devil seen in picture books, complete with red tights and a loosely-fitting red shirt. In his hand was a large, sharp-bladed ax. Our eyes briefly met. His cocky smile revealed a certain arrogance as he gleefully chopped down the tree branch by branch until only a stump remained. As he worked, branches were strewn far and wide upon the forest floor with a kind of condescending satisfaction. As he let out a disturbing cackle, our eyes met briefly for a second time. The smirk on his face told me he had taken pleasure in his destructive achievement. I watched in silence as he slowly swaggered away, disappearing into the forest, but not before he turned around one more time, giving me a last glimpse of this gloating smile.

I was left standing forlorn in my grief among the broken branches. My sorrow was compounded by the adversary's enjoyment of his devastation. Why would he mock me the way he did? The tree, which was meant to be whole and green and beautiful, was left in pieces, like my heart. Mirroring the brokenness of our family, each branch represented a brother, sister, aunt, uncle, mother, or father. One small branch represented me. I stood like a silent statue, lost and bewildered. Many life events had ravaged my family over the years. Relationships had been broken. Some were never reconciled.

The vision continued. Seemingly out of nowhere, there appeared a white-robed man, entering the scene from the right. This gentler, kinder sort of fellow, with a welcoming smile, walked slowly toward me. I watched as His eyes scanned the devastation. He seemed to be looking for something specific, as he passed several branches lying on the ground. Eventually, He came upon one branch that was about a foot and a half long, jagged on both ends. I can't tell you how I knew, but it was obvious that this particular branch represented me. He held it out as if to draw my attention to it. Then He tightly clutched the branch in one hand, quickly and firmly plunging it into His own heart. I gasped in horror! Why would He do such a thing? Why would He willingly inflict such pain upon His body? For a moment there was only silence as I pondered what seemed like such a dreadfully painful act. And then He spoke to me in reassuring tones.

"There! Now, you are part of My family. I have planted you in My heart; grafted you in, and you belong to Me."

I stood amazed by this act of kindness and the profound sense of belonging it created deep within me. Healing love was at work, melting the sadness and sorrow caused by the evil one's destruction. Wholeheartedly, I embraced my position in God's family. He had rescued, adopted, and welcomed me into His heart.

My former emotional pain was gone. In its place was a comforting sense of belonging and a renewed confidence in my belovedness. God seemed to lovingly say, *"You are worth rescuing. You are valued as a person. You are a part of My family: a whole, healed, 'perfected-in-love' kind of family. Lean into that. Receive it with your entire heart, soul, and mind. Though your earthly family is broken, your heavenly family is capable of fully embracing you with everlasting kindness."*

Moving Toward Knowing Our True Selves By Embracing The Whole Self

Knowing ourselves as God sees us and knowing God for who He truly is go hand in hand. That's why so much of this book is dedicated to these two topics. One doesn't happen without the other. Many fathers of our faith recognized this same truth. You were introduced to Thomas Merton's thoughts on this subject in the quote at the beginning of this chapter. Here are a few more examples:

- Thomas a Kempis (late 1300s-1400s) argued that "a humble self-knowledge is a surer way to God than a search after deep learning."[13]
- Augustine's (354-430 AD) prayer was, "Grant, Lord, that I may know myself, that I may know Thee."[14]
- John Calvin's (1500s) opening words in the *Institutes of the Christian Religion* were "There is no deep knowing of God without a deep knowing of self and no deep knowing of self without a deep knowing of God."[15]

In the previous chapter we took time to explore some of our false beliefs. Now, let's begin the adventure of getting to know ourselves as we truly are: our "true selves."

We take a giant step toward wholeness when we embrace all that is true about ourselves: the acceptable and beautiful as well as the unacceptable or unlovely aspects of our nature. In the beginning, there is value in becoming aware of and naming some of the excluded or hidden parts of one's self; the parts that are true about you but that you would rather disown. You might even ask a friend or family member you feel safe with what you are like on your good days and bad days. It might look something like this:

Activity: Naming What Is True About Me On My Best And Worst Days

On My Best Days	On My Worst Days
My playful self	My cautious (untrusting) self
My creative self	My anxious self
My caring self	My angry self
My organized self	

My motivated self	My serious self
My self-reflective self	My people-pleasing self
My humble self	My competitive self
My inquisitive self	My overwhelmed self
My relational self	My self-absorbed self
My thoughtful self	My unmotivated self
	My insecure self

It's important to remember that God loves and embraces us on both our best and worst days. He accepts us as we are, but He doesn't leave us there. His desire for us is healing and wholeness. We are always in process on this dynamic adventure with Him, and His abiding, loving presence is strong and powerful. He is our loving Father, our kind Shepherd, and our faithful Friend, patiently walking and working with us.

We all have good and bad days, strengths and weaknesses, desirable traits and undesirable ones. Part of our healing and wholeness come as we accept our true selves: the selves we are when we put our best foot forward and the selves we are when we're stressed and exhausted.

Early in childhood we begin to develop strategies for ensuring that our basic needs are met. Thomas Merton calls these our "programs for happiness." They are our needs for:

- Safety and survival
- Power and control
- Esteem and approval (love)

As toddlers, our caregivers clap, smile, and give us lots of praise (approval) when we take our first steps, learn to throw a ball in their direction, or share toys with another child. And so it begins. On the other hand, we may experience disapproval or loss of control when we hear the word "No!" or get our hand slapped when we do something our caregivers disapprove of like touching a hot stove. We learn quickly that some things are welcomed and some things are disapproved of. We may even make the false assumption that we are either good or bad because of what we do or don't do. We usually opt for doing what is approved of as long as it gets our needs met in one of the three core areas listed above.

What we don't know is that our need for safety, power, and approval will never be fully met in this lifetime, and especially not in the ways we may try to get them met. As adults we may strive to attain status, earn more money, look good on the outside, or engage in people-pleasing. No matter how adept we are at achieving these aims, they will never help us feel fully satisfied or at home with our true selves.

We also look for ways of protecting ourselves, covering up or hiding our unacceptable parts so others won't hurt or reject us. But all the effort we expend covering up what we don't want seen is futile. We may manage to hide for a while, but we can't maintain the facade indefinitely. It's like painting a car with water-based paint so it looks like new. When it begins to rain, the thin layer of paint will run or peel off. Eventually, who we really are becomes obvious.

There are also parts of ourselves that we may not be aware of, but just because they are hidden from us does not mean others can't see them. For example, we may have a core of shame but refuse to look at it or accept it because it's too painful. However, those who know us may detect our insecurities by the fact that we either push them away or that we seem uncomfortable around them.

So, how do we know when we are living more or less out of our true selves? When we are living out of our **false selves,** we tend to be fearful, overly protective, possessive, manipulative, controlling, destructive, self-promoting, indulgent, insecure, or entitled. By contrast, when we're living out of our **true selves,** we usually display characteristics of freedom, acceptance, compassion, love, and union with God. The challenge is to get unstuck from where we are so we can live life more fully and freely out of our true selves.

Developing a relationship of intimacy with God enables us to grow in the knowledge of who we really are in Christ. The more we get to know God experientially, the more we are able to understand how God sees us and names us. We can best know and embrace our true selves by walking day by day in the love and light of God's grace. Pursuing greater intimacy with God also helps us uncover all the lies the world and the enemy of our souls, Satan, have placed upon us. Part of pursuing intimacy with God happens as we search out and meditate on Scripture passages that affirm who we truly are. Another part of pursuing intimacy is doing deep soul work to uncover what may be causing us to stay stuck.

Doing The Work

Activity: Distinguishing Between The True And False Self

Take a look at the chart below and consider the traits that are mostly true about you and the ways you relate to others around you. Put a check mark by all that apply. Be as honest as you can. This is between you and God, and He already knows the truth. Once you've completed this activity you should have a better idea of where some of your stuck-ness resides. Then move on to the next activity.

Characteristics of Living out of the *False Self*	Characteristics of Living out of the *True Self*
· Fearful · Protective · Possessive · Manipulative · Controlling · Destructive · Self-promoting · Indulgent · Entitled	· Free · Accepting · Joyful · Compassionate · Loving · Forgiving · Trusting · One with God

Embracing Truth With Grace And Gentleness

It's important to be gentle with ourselves as we progress toward wholeness. Remember, it's usually a slow process, requiring much patience. God deeply desires that we come to know ourselves as He knows us, but this usually takes more time than we'd like. John Mark Comer writes that "Hurry is the enemy of spiritual growth."[16] Allow God, slowly over time, to reveal areas in your life where you may believe a lie that keeps you from moving forward into freedom.

One of the strategies that has helped me and those I have had the privilege of working with is something I call **Exchanging Truth for Lies**. Do this activity repeatedly, as a practice, until the truths become embedded in your heart and mind. Since our brains are pliable, we can develop new neural pathways. Through repetition the brain can rewire itself and, in so doing, change the way it perceives things. Where once you automatically felt unloved, with practice you can learn to believe you are loved. With practice, you will move closer and closer to living more confidently and naturally as the person God has always intended you to be, assured of His unending, extravagant love and friendship.

Activity: Exchanging Truth For Lies

1. First, choose a word or phrase that seems connected to an emotional wound or a *past* negative experience, such as defective, worthless, unlovable, not enough, etc. Refer back to the previous chapter's chart of negative messages for words and phrases that carry an emotional charge.

2. Next, choose an opposite, positive, or replacement word that reflects the way God sees you. A word may naturally come to your mind, or you may want to use the **True Identity in Christ** chart provided further below.

3. Use a Bible concordance to look up your new word and find a Scripture reference to back up what God says is true about you.

4. Then, think of one or two feeling words that describe how you feel about the truth of how God sees you.

Example:

Negative Word or Phrase	God's Truth	Scripture Reference and/or Verse	Feeling Words
Worthless	Highly Favored	*"Let not steadfast love and faithfulness forsake you…so you will find favor in the sight of God and man"* (Proverbs 3:3-4, ESV) *"For His anger is for a moment and His favor is for a lifetime"* (Psalm 30:5).	Encouraged Hopeful Valued
Defective	Complete in Him	*"…He has given us His very great and precious promises, so that through them you may participate in the divine*	Confident Grateful

		nature..." (2 Peter 1:4).	
Unlovable	His Beloved Delighted in	"You will be called by a new name that the mouth of the Lord will bestow. You will be a crown of splendor in the Lord's hand, a royal diadem in the hand of your God. No longer will they call you Deserted or name your land Desolate; but you will be called, 'My delight is in you,' for the Lord will take delight in you" (Isaiah 62:2b-4).	Loved Cherished

My True Identity In Christ

The True Self

Abba's child (Galatians 4:6, Romans 8:15) **Accepted in the beloved** (Ephesians 1:6) **Adopted** (Galatians 4:5) **Always in His thoughts** (Isaiah 49:15) **Anointed** (I John 2:27) **Apple of His eye** (Zechariah 2:8) **Becoming mature & complete, (transformed)** (2 Corinthians 3:18) **His beloved** (Psalm 60:5, NKJV)	**Cherished** (Ephesians 5:29) **Comforted, as a mother comforts her child** (Isaiah 66:13) **Complete through union with Him** (Colossians 2:9-10) **Confident** (Proverbs 3:26) **Crowned with glory, compassion, love, and honor** (Psalm 8:5, Psalm 103:4) **Delighted in** (Psalm 16:3, Zephaniah 3:17)

Blessed with every spiritual blessing (Ephesians 1:3)	**Fearfully and wonderfully made** (Psalm 139:13 and 14)
His bride (Isaiah 54:5)	**Forgiven** (Jeremiah 31:34, Micah 7:19)
Cared for with compassion (Isaiah 46:3 -4, 1 Peter 5:2)	**Free from condemnation** (Romans 8:1)
Called according to His purpose (Romans 8:28 & Psalm 138:8)	**God's workmanship (handiwork, masterpiece)** (Ephesians 2:10)
Carried (Isaiah 46:4)	**Having authority to overcome** (1 John 5:4 ESV)
Chosen (John 15:16)	**Heir of God** (Galatians 3:29)
	Light of the world (Matthew 5:14)

Scripture Verses To Read, Pray, Memorize, Or Meditate On

I have called you by name, you are Mine. — Isaiah 43:1b, RSV

See, I have engraved you on the palms of My hands... (Isaiah 49:16).

Nothing between us and God, our faces shining with the brightness of His face. And so, we are transfigured much like the Messiah, our lives gradually becoming brighter and more beautiful as God enters our lives and we become like Him. -- 2 Corinthians 3:18, MSG

"For we are God's masterpiece. He has created us anew in Christ Jesus, so we can do the good things He planned for us long ago". – Ephesians 2:10, NLT

The King James Version says,

The LORD thy God in the midst of thee (is) mighty, he will save, he will rejoice over thee with joy; he will rest in his love, he will joy over thee with joy; he will rest in his love, he will joy over thee with singing. – Zephaniah 3:17

This same passage below was beautifully paraphrased by Dennis Jernigan.

The eternal self-existent God, the God who is three in one. He who dwells in the center of your being is a powerful and valiant warrior.

He has come to set you free, to keep you safe and to bring you victory. He is cheered and He beams with exceeding joy and takes pleasure in your presence.

He has engraved a place for Himself in you and there He quietly rests in His love and affection for you. He cannot contain Himself at the thought of you and with the greatest joy spins around wildly in anticipation over you...and has placed you above all other creations and in the highest place in His priorities.

In fact, He shouts and sings in triumph joyfully proclaiming the gladness of His heart in a song of rejoicing!

All because of you![17]

Pause and meditate: Is there a new name God seems to be giving you?

Questions And Activities To Take You Deeper (Choose One Or More)

Activity #1: Scripture Meditation-A New Name Read the following Scripture again slowly and thoughtfully. Do you have a sense of how God may be naming you today? If so, journal about it below, and then write your new name on a card or on a rock, and place it in a prominent place in your home. Return to that "new name" often to remind yourself of how God sees you.

> *... you will be called by a new name that the mouth of the Lord will bestow. You will be a crown of splendor in the Lord's hand, and a royal diadem in the hand of your God. No longer will they call you Deserted, or name your land Desolate. But you will be called Hephzibah (My delight is in her); and your land Beulah (Married); for the Lord will take delight in you.*
> *—Isaiah 62:2-4a*

Activity #2: Journal Reflection Reflecting on the truths you've discovered about yourself and about God in this chapter, journal an affirming statement, a letter of gratitude to Jesus, or a letter to yourself from Jesus. Perhaps you'd like to thank Him for the ways He has revealed His love toward you through Scripture and your time of meditating on Him. You might want to celebrate the enlightened understanding you've found in experiencing His love more profoundly or on a deeper level. Let God's Spirit and your own creativity guide you as you write.

Activity #3: A Spiritual Practice Are there areas of your life you wish to lift up to God for healing, restoration, or His nurturing touch? If so, spend a few moments sharing those areas with God. You may want to use the process outlined below, "*Listening, Disclosing, Absorbing, Reflecting, Responding, and Giving* It may help you be more aware of God's presence and work in your life. Consider using a journal as you complete the following practice. This practice can be done in one extended sitting. It may also be used in a half-day personal or small group retreat. If your time is limited, you might want to do this over two or three days.

_____

_____

_____

_____

_____

Spiritual Practice: Prayer As Listening, Disclosing, Absorbing, Reflecting, Responding, And Giving

Begin by breathing slowly and deeply, yet comfortably, giving God permission to work and access the deepest places of your heart.

Listening: Open your heart to God by becoming inwardly still and receptive to what He may want to show you. Continue breathing softly as you center on God's presence. Next, tune into your thoughts, feelings, and inclinations. What (negative or positive) is going on inside you? What do you want or need from God? What would you like to say to Him? Spend a few minutes in quiet listening, centering on God's presence.

Disclosing: We reveal ourselves just as we are to God in prayer by sharing our thoughts, feelings, and desires with Him. This may include sharing with God a negative label or situations from our past. It may include a more recent disturbing situation, thought, or emotion. Share that area of concern with God verbally in prayer or in your journal.

Note: *It's not that God is unaware of your concerns, but disclosing to Him helps us see and name what is going on more clearly and not feel like we need to hide it from God. Naming our negative thoughts and feelings can help neutralize them. It also helps to begin a two-way conversation where we feel known and heard. This ongoing conversation cultivates intimacy with God.*

If nothing is troubling you at the moment, you can simply affirm your love and gratitude for the many positive things in your life currently. This practice isn't just for times of struggle or pain. It can also draw us closer to God during times of celebration and thanksgiving.

Absorbing: We become more deeply connected to God by allowing Him to disclose Himself to us through Scripture as He opens up its meaning to us personally. Additional ways we hear from God are through dreams, visions, other people, promptings, an audible voice (very rarely), worship music, repeated instances, or a persistent sense of something. How would you like to open your heart more fully to the presence of God right now?

Surrender to Him as you sit in His presence. Ask Him to speak to you. Be open to the way He chooses to be with you.

Reflecting: We deepen our experience of God by becoming more and more aware of how God meets us in our daily lives. We can do this by reviewing the current day or the previous day, noticing how God has been present in its events and emotions. As you pause in the silence, consider where you have felt loved or given love, joy, beauty, or encouragement. List those ways. Also consider where you felt the absence of love, joy, beauty, or encouragement. List the things that come to mind. Next, reflect on the ways God was or is present to you in both feeling loved (for example) and not feeling loved.

Today I felt God's love (joy, beauty, encouragement) when...	I felt the absence of God's love (joy beauty, encouragement) when...
1.	1.
2.	2.

It's easier, of course, to sense God's presence in the positive things. However, we can also sense God's presence in negative experiences. Here's an example: I was with a friend who was grieving the eventual loss of her friend who was dying. She was overcome by sadness and grief. As we talked together, she became encouraged by how God had been using her to bring joy to her hospitalized friend. My friend's perspective on the situation changed as she saw herself partnering with the Trinity to bring joy to that hospital room.

Responding: We learn to follow God's leading or the promptings that come as a result of reflecting. Then, we respond through obedience and submission. You might sense a prompting to send someone an encouraging card or text message. We can affirm our love, faith, and trust in God by thanking Him for His good gifts to us. How would you like to respond to God in this moment? Journal or offer up a prayer of gratitude. Is there anything else God is inviting you to do as a response to your experience of His presence or prompting today?

_____

_____

_____

_____

Giving: We freely offer to others the gifts we have received by sharing God's love and spreading His kingdom in our community and in the world. How have you shared kindness toward someone you know or given a gift lately? As I was typing this section, my husband came into the room to give me a freshly peeled tangerine. I was delighted and thanked him for responding to God's prompting! I also thanked him for his impeccable timing. I was getting hungry! Consider how God might be leading you to lovingly give to someone who needs something you have to offer. How can you show someone you care for them, this week?

_____

_____

_____

_____

Each of the activities above requires intention and practice. The more we engage in them, the more God and His goodness will grow and become a natural part of our thought life.

How Does God Change Us?

We come to know our true selves by looking into the face of Jesus, by noticing how He names us and how He truly sees us, and by allowing Him to exchange the lies we believe for truth. Think of the way a newborn baby looks into its mother's face and reflects her smile. The baby is developing a positive sense of self. I love to watch as my four-month-old grandson looks into my daughter's smiling face. He responds with a smile that seems to light up the room. I invite you to spend time looking into your heavenly Father's face. See His love reflected toward you as He delights in you.

> *Nothing between us and God, our faces shining with the brightness of His face. And so, we are transfigured much like the Messiah, our lives gradually becoming brighter and more beautiful as God enters our lives and we become like Him.*
> *—2 Corinthians 3:18, MSG*

It's commonly known that we often become like the people we spend the most time with. When we make space and turn our focus to God through a spiritual practice, we give him the opportunity to do His work in us.

Nuggets For The Journey

I invite you to enjoy two offerings: a prayer by Saint Catherine of Siena and a poem by Hafiz e Shiraz. May they be an encouragement along the path toward intimacy with God.

> You, O eternal Trinity, are a deep sea, into which the more I enter the more I find, and the more I find the more I seek... O eternal Godhead, what more could You give me than Yourself? You are the fire that ever burns without being consumed: You consume in Your heat all the soul's self-love; You are the fire which takes away cold; with Your light You illuminate me, so that I may know all Your truth.
> —St. Catherine of Siena, 1347-1380[18]

It Felt Love
by Hafiz e Shiraz

How
Did the rose
Ever open its heart
And give to this world
All its
Beauty?
It felt the encouragement of light
Against its
Being.
Otherwise,
We all remain
Too
Frightened.[19]

7 THE PURPOSE OF THE PRACTICES

Creating Space For God

"What repeatedly enters your mind and occupies your mind, eventually shapes your mind, and will ultimately express itself in what you do and who you become."

—JOHN ORTBERG

La Sagrada Familia - A Place Of Rebirthing

"Even the moon was embarrassed by the beauty of Barcelona."
—*Andrew Barger*

In the heart of Barcelona near the famous old bullfighting stadium, which had been turned into a multi-level shopping mall, stood our quaint hotel. It was less than a half a block from La Rambla, the most famous street in all of Barcelona. The tree-lined avenue was brightly lit; perfect for romantic evening walks. Our spiritual pilgrimage through Spain was about to begin, seeking more of God in some of the beautiful, spiritually-oriented places in this colorful city.

After a good night's sleep, we embarked upon three days of artistic, cultural, and spiritual discovery. Little did we know that our visit to the unfinished Roman Catholic Basilica de la Sagrada Familia, Barcelona's signature emblem, would provide us with treasured memories of a lifetime. Once inside the world-famous basilica, we delighted in the warm afternoon sunlight as it shone through colorful stained-glass windows. The light cast a kaleidoscope of rainbow colors on the floor of the great basilica. From every angle the church was aglow with artistic delights. Like giant tree trunks, the massive granite and basalt pillars stood tall, touching the vaulted ceiling. Each pillar was aglow with brilliant colors reflected through the stained glass. The whole sanctuary was engulfed in awe-inspiring beauty.

I spotted ElRoy sitting quietly on a stone bench on the opposite side of the room. Walking toward him, we both smiled. I commented on the wonder of such a magnificent synergy of light, color, and design, "Isn't this amazing?" He nodded, peaceful and relaxed, immersed in the grandeur of what he, too, was experiencing. Sitting silently next to him, I continued to soak in the beautiful essence from a spot where I could enjoy this architectural marvel.

As I took a more thoughtful look at the colors along the far wall, I saw that the warm glow cast by the window's reds, oranges, and yellows created a bright, lively floral design, resembling large yellow sunflowers with orange centers. By contrast, on the opposite side of the room the window's greens, purples, and blues cast their cool glow on the many pillars, designed to look like enormous tree trunks with a ceiling canopy of branches and leaves. From this angle the room resembled an enchanted, elfin forest. It was like we had morphed into a long-ago time of fantasy and fairies! For several minutes I simply sat quietly, immersed in the glory of colorful images all around me.

"A place that could fill the mind, heart, and soul with such delight must contain a gift for those who can perceive it," I thought. This imaginative place, where creativity and nature are mingled with spirituality, breathed new life into me.

The longer I sat the more I began to sense the presence of God surrounding me, gently drawing me closer. I felt lighter, yet deeper in, toward the comforting heart of God. As my eyes closed, surprisingly, a vision began to play in my mind's eye. As I sat riveted on my cool, granite slab, the oval-shaped room began to change, appearing as a living organism: a semi-clear, large oval shape, resembling a bodily organ. Intrigued and a bit confused, I wondered what this emerging shape might be. *"Was there some kind of message for me?"* With my eyes still closed, I watched in awe as this strange object continued taking shape. What had been the tall red and orange pillars of the Sagrada Familia now thinned out and lengthened, taking on the look of veins and arteries running through the body. They bent themselves around and through the soft, life-like shape. Then I heard a subtle thumping sound, like a softly beating drum. As I listened more intently, it seemed to be the beating of a heart. Strangely, I felt like I was a part of this soft, life-like image; as though I were actually encased in it. I wondered if the image could be a mother's womb or her heart, and what that might mean for me.

As I sat pondering and questioning, I wondered, *"Could this be Mary's womb? Was I encircled by it, close enough to hear her heartbeat?"* It seemed a little *out there*—fantastical—and quite puzzling.

Time stood still as I tried to discern the meaning this heavenly visitation might have for me. A warm, nurturing sensation came over me. Though the vision seemed unusual, it calmed and comforted me. I felt protected and tenderly held, as if by Divine love. I had never heard or read of anything like this happening to anyone. Though the message was still somewhat unclear, my sense was that God had something profound to show me.

For almost two days, I spoke to no one about what had happened. Some things seem too sacred to speak of. Yet I continued reflecting on the vision and spent time in God's presence, asking for clarity and discernment. As I revisited and reimagined this experience, holding it safely in my heart, a familiar Scripture passage emerged in my memory.

> *You formed my innermost being, shaping my delicate inside and my intricate outside, and wove them all together in my mother's womb...You even formed every bone in my body when you created me in the secret place; carefully, skillfully You shaped me from nothing to something. You saw who You created me to be before I became me! Before I'd ever seen the light of day, the number of days You planned for me were already recorded in Your book.*
> *—Psalm 139:13-16*

My heart listened closely as God impressed upon me the understanding that He was rebirthing me as His child. As part of this spiritual rebirthing, God seemed to be affirming that He was knitting me together with His love. His intimate presence would continue to repair and heal the childhood wounds that were a result of the imperfect love of my own mother. His nurturing love would be a pathway toward wholeness and the freedom to be my true self. He was softening the childhood pain and replacing it with an experience of His nurturing love. In the process, I was becoming better acquainted with the more feminine qualities of God.

The knowledge of this revelation filled me with deep joy and satisfaction. I was at home with myself, and felt compassionately held. Throughout the remainder of our pilgrimage, I revisited this experience in my imagination. While reengaging with the vision, I allowed myself the space to spend a few encouraging minutes daily bathing in the awareness of God's nurturing presence with me by meditating on a few verses of Psalm 139:

> *Every single moment you are thinking of me! How precious and wonderful to consider that you cherish me constantly in your every thought! O God, your desires toward me are more than grains of sand on every shore! When I awake each morning, you're still with me.*
> *—Psalm 139:17-18, TPT*

God seemed to be whispering to me,

"Though your mother was unable to nurture you, I will never leave or forsake you. I am rebirthing you into a life of beauty and goodness. You are my beloved child, whom I love with everlasting compassion. I look upon you with joy and delight. Your life with me will bring healing and restoration. Rest, in that assurance."

What Are Spiritual Practices/Disciplines, And Why Do We Need Them?

Spiritual practices, or disciplines, are ways of being with God, *making space* in our hearts for Him and becoming one with Him. Saint Teresa of Avila, a fourteenth-century Spanish Carmelite nun, prominent Spanish mystic, and religious reformer, put it this way: "The point is that we should make a gift of our hearts, emptying them of ourselves, that they may be filled with God. Our Almighty Father becomes one with us and transforms us, uniting Creator and creature. How desirable is this union!"

Spiritual disciplines are a means of grace, pathways to transformation. By grace I am referring to God's work in us to change us or transform us from the inside out. God, through His grace and power, forms our inner being and changes us into the kind of person who loves as He loves, has inward joy, and has a deep peace, just as He has. Through grace, God does what cannot be done by our effort alone. By practicing the disciplines, we put ourselves in a place where the Spirit can train us to be like Jesus in character and in deed. We grow in Christlike character, and we have access through the Holy Spirit to God's power to do good work in the world.

_____

_____

_____

_____

_____

We don't simply coast into Christian maturity.

Growth into Christlikeness involves effort. "We need to be intentional in our practice of the disciplines. Holiness is not a condition into which we drift." writes John Stott.[20]

As Dallas Willard famously stated, "Grace is not opposed to effort, it is opposed to earning. Earning is an attitude. Effort is an action."[21] Dallas emphasized the importance of deliberately choosing to be a disciple of Jesus. A disciple is someone who decides to walk with Jesus as His apprentice, in an effort to learn to be more like Him.

As Willard also wrote, "A disciple is a person who has decided that the most important thing in their life is to learn to do what Jesus said to do."[22]

An important aspect of discipleship is having access to activities (tools), such as practices that support spiritual transformation into the likeness of Christ. By God's grace and through the use of spiritual practices, we give God access to our hearts, as He changes and forms us from the inside out.

Spiritual practices are not really the goal or the end in themselves. It is not the practices that transform us, nor are they the only way we are transformed. God also works through life situations, especially suffering and difficult relationships, to transform our character to be more like His. Though the practices are helpful tools, we are encouraged not to make spiritual formation just about the practices/disciplines. Spiritual formation, maturity, and wholeness are more about a life of surrender to God. We then become the kind of person God is able to communicate with and communicate through. It's about becoming our true selves, persons whom God created to live life fully and love others well.

Our Spiritual Pathways Can Guide Us

You might be wondering; how do we know which practices are right or best for us? We will likely prefer some practices over others. The Spiritual Pathways Test, as recommended by Gary Thomas in his book *Sacred Pathways*,[23] can help you determine your strongest spiritual pathways. Simply Google "Spiritual Pathways Test" and take one of the assessments listed there. You will receive your results almost immediately. There are several versions of this assessment. Any of them can be helpful in guiding your understanding of how different practices naturally fall in line with a specific pathway. You will most likely be attracted to the practices that align with your top three pathways. Determine which pathways seem to help you *most naturally* connect with God. It was helpful for me to determine that my top three pathways were Nature, Sensate, and Intellectual. Since Nature was my top pathway, I knew it would be important for me to connect with God through His creation. Or I might want to sit by a large window as I engaged in my morning quiet time.

Reflect on the list below of spiritual pathways from Gary Thomas' book. Can you tell even without taking the assessment which pathways you feel most drawn to? Remember, there are several versions of this assessment on the internet and elsewhere, and most of them don't include all of the pathways. Your results will vary slightly depending on which test you take.

> **The Naturalist** enjoys, experiences, and draws near to God by being out in nature or bringing aspects of nature inside.
>
> **The Relational** person enjoys, experiences, and draws near to God through others, engaging in self-disclosure, having deep, rich relationships, hearing God's voice through others.
>
> **The Worshiper** enjoys, experiences, and draws near to God through corporate and private worship.

The Contemplative enjoys, experiences, and draws near to God by immersing themselves in prayer and setting aside time for personal adoration of God and heartfelt devotion to Him.

The Activist enjoys, experiences, and draws near to God best while waging war on injustice and maintaining a single-minded zeal to accomplish God's cause in the world.

The Intellectual enjoys, experiences, and draws near to God best through study and other forms of using the mind and growing in knowledge.

The Service oriented person enjoys, experiences, and draws near to God best when performing concrete tasks for God and others. They may have the spiritual gifts of "helps."

The Sensate enjoys, experiences, and draws near to God best through their five senses (touch, taste, sight, hearing, and smell).

The Traditionalist enjoys, experiences, and draws near to God best through ritual and symbol.

The Ascetic enjoys, experiences, and draws near to God best through solitude and simplicity.

The Caregiver enjoys, experiences, and draws near to God best through caring for and serving others.

The Enthusiast enjoys, experiences, and draws near to God best through celebration and mystery.[24]

Once you determine your top two or three pathways, you will be able to decide which specific practices fall under those categories. These practices will most generally be key in your efforts toward connection with God. In order to move toward wholeness, however, it is also wise to spend some time cultivating the pathways and practices that come *less naturally* to you. For instance, a person who has a strong relational pathway usually loves community and connects easily to God through involvement in community, but can also benefit from spending time alone in quiet and solitude with God. A person who loves spending quiet time alone with God also needs to learn to share with others on a deeper level and to be a part of a safe and loving community. The rule of thumb is to lean into the practices you find most helpful or are naturally attracted to, but also choose a few practices that support and encourage growth in weaker areas of your spiritual life.

Spiritual practices help us become more aware of and available to God so that He can do His transforming work in us. They open us up to God's loving healing presence. A quote by Doug Gregg, founder of CFDM Christian Formation Direction Ministries, explains the purpose of the practices and why they are so effective in our lives: "It is not our control and practice of the disciplines that makes a difference, but our yielding to the power and influence of the Holy Spirit through the practice of the disciplines, that gives Him (God) space to speak to us and guide us, to fill us and empower us, to turn us around."[25]

Here are some specific ways the practices allow God and His Spirit to do His work in us:
  * Some practices help us *pay attention* to what God is doing.

Noticing, Prayer of Examen, Slowing, Silence, Nature Walks, Solitude
  * Some practices help us *process* what God is doing.

Journaling, Prayer of Examen, Reflection, Welcoming Prayer

- Some practices help us *become more aware* of God's presence.

All of the practices

- Some practices help us *become more responsive* to God's invitations to us.

Surrender, Examination of Conscience, Meditation, Devotional Reading, Retreat

A rule of thumb: Pray as you can, not as you can't.

Embrace this freedom as an invitation, rather than a demand.

What Kinds Of Activities Can Be A Practice?

There are many "traditional" practices. Adele Ahlberg Calhoun's excellent book, *Spiritual Disciplines Handbook: Practices That Transform Us*, details 75 spiritual practices.[26] Most of them were used through the centuries. Other activities could be categorized as spiritual practices. A key to deciding whether something is a spiritual practice is discerning whether the action or activity actually helps you be with or be mindful of God, or aids you in getting to know Him better. For example, doing the dishes, laundry, gardening, etc. could be used as practices, if the person doing them is focused on Jesus washing away our worries or exchanging our negative thoughts to more kingdom-of-God thoughts. I sometimes use a simple Breath Prayer while watering my plants. As I move from one plant to the next, I repeat a short phrase like, *"Lord, nourish my soul with Your Living Water."* Sometimes I just listen to worship music or express gratitude as I do a specific task.

Authors Brother Lawrence and Frank C. Laubach have both written books on the topic of practicing the presence of God in every moment while completing everyday tasks. When we regularly engage in spiritual practices, we naturally become more and more aware of God's presence with us in all of life.

Many classical practices have been used for centuries and handed down for our use today. Here is a list of a few of these practices presented in Adele Calhoun's book with a brief description of each one. Some may be familiar to you and some may be new. This is only a small portion of the total number presented in Calhoun's book.[27]

Spiritual Discipline	Description
Bible Study	Engaging the mind and focusing the attention on Scripture in an attempt to understand and apply truth to every part of life
Breath Prayer	A form of contemplative prayer linked to the rhythms of breathing. (1) Breathe in, calling on a Biblical name or Image of God, and (2) Breathe out a simple God-given desire.
Celebration	A way of engaging in actions that orient my spirit toward worship and thanksgiving. Delighting in all the attentions and never-changing presence of the Trinity fuels celebration.
Contemplative Prayer	A receptive posture of openness toward God; a way of waiting with a heart awake to God's presence and His Word. This kind of prayer

	intentionally trusts and rests.
Devotional Reading	Requires an open reflective, listening posture alert to the voice of God; is aimed more at growing in relationship with God than gathering information about God.
Prayer of Examen	A practice for discerning the voice and activity of God within the flow of the day. A vehicle that creates deeper awareness of God-given desires in one's life.
Forgiveness	To live into Jesus' forgiving heart and stop the cycle of vengeance.
Gratitude	A loving and thankful response toward God for His presence with us and within the world. Delight in God and His good will is the heartbeat of thankfulness.
Inner-Healing Prayer	Invites those with emotional wounds to enter the presence of Jesus and to open themselves to listen to Him and his Words to them as they seek wholeness and freedom
Journaling	A tool for reflecting on God's presence, guidance, and nurture in daily comings and goings. Journals can be kept regularly or during times of transition.
Listening Prayer/ Lectio Divina	Allows God to set the agenda for prayer and respond to the word that is given or read.
Meditation	An ardent (passionate) gaze at God, His work, and His Word.
Prayer of Recollection	A restful attitude of connecting with the reality that God is in me. As we let go of distractions, this prayer recalls the soul to its true center and identity in Christ.
Rest	Depends on honoring our God-given limits. By paying attention to the physical, mental, and spiritual needs of the body we learn when and how to rest.
Retreat	Specific, regular times set apart for quietly listening to God and delighting in His company. Retreats remove us from the daily battle into times of refreshing, retooling, renewing, and unwinding.
Rule of Life	Sometimes called Rhythm of Life. To live a sane and holy rhythm that reflects a deep love for God and respect for how He has made me.
Slowing	Is one way to overcome inner hurriedness and addiction to business. Through slowing, the sacrament of the present moment is tasted to the full.
Visio Divina	To worship God in the beauty of created things such as art, sculpture, nature, etc.

You may have already discovered that you can do a certain practice, yet your mind is somewhere else completely. Think of times you've been driving your car and you "wake up" or become fully aware on the way to your destination and think, *"Wow, I haven't been fully conscious of my driving."* Or maybe you've even arrived at a certain destination but you can't remember how you got there. That kind of thing has happened to me more than once. Let's say you're trying to meditate on a passage of Scripture but your mind is preoccupied with the fact that you have dishes in the sink or yard work to do. Having your Bible open to a specific Scripture isn't doing you any good unless you are present to what you are reading, and present to God. Focusing our minds and attention on God is key to whether the practice is effective, and if we're even engaged in the practice at all.

Usually, some mental preparation is helpful before engaging in a spiritual practice. This helps ensure that you are fully present in the moment. You might have a specific chair in a certain room, or a corner of a room decorated with a candle, flowers, an essential oil diffuser, pleasing artwork or sacred symbols on the wall to make the area more conducive to drawing closer to God. In our home we have a room dedicated to spending quality time with God and for doing spiritual direction. This room contains a comfortable leather chair and a small white couch. The walls are covered with murals of trees and flowers. One painting depicts a scene from the Bible, and additional sacred symbols encourage quiet meditation and focus on God.

Remember that though the practices are important, it isn't the practices that transform us. We are transformed through our surrendered response and obedience to God as we engage with Him through the practices. In so doing we facilitate an inner change leading to us, over time, to become more like Jesus.

Incorporating the disciplines into our lives is like learning any new skill. My first time riding my big, blue bike with two-inch-thick tires was a challenge. Even with training wheels I felt awkward as I wobbled slowly down the sidewalk, my grandfather holding onto the back of the seat to steady me. Then the training wheels came off. It took a while for me to get comfortable starting, stopping, and balancing on that bike, but at long last I could ride confidently by myself. Learning to drive a car with a stick shift was equally awkward. Spiritual practices can sometimes feel unusual or awkward in the beginning. That's why we *practice* them. The more comfortable we become with the practices, the more easily we will begin to see their benefits and delight in the ways God draws us closer through them.

Jesus invites us to experience His purposes for us with freedom and individuality. We have so many practices at our disposal. I like to think of this as a well-stocked toolbox or kitchen. You choose the tool that best fits your current need. God can use any of the practices to draw us closer to Him and to help us enter into a restorative, nurturing place.

As you consider incorporating a particular practice into your life, consider who you are and where you are on your journey. Pay attention to your life's season, your needs, your desires, and your particular spiritual pathways.

Reading For Transformation

In my earlier years as I first began to seek a more intimate relationship with God, I used the practice of Lectio Divina, meaning "divine reading," to help me better understand the true nature of God. This practice called for the reading of a short passage of Scripture (four to eight verses) three or four times, slowly. With each reading the truths presented in the verses sunk deeper and deeper into my being. Reading God's Word slowly, thoughtfully, and prayerfully changed me. It literally transformed my mind, creating new neural pathways of belief and understanding.

If the scriptural content was about God's character—for example, about His compassion—I became more and more conscious of God's loving, compassionate presence with me personally at increasingly deeper levels. I began to feel grounded in who He really was as my loving Father. It also affirmed who I was as His beloved daughter. The information I read went from an intellectual-knowing, or "head-knowledge," to an experiential-knowing, or "heart-knowledge." Once I became comfortable reading Scripture in this way, with a focus on experiencing God intimately, I was more able to access His healing love and acceptance. Throughout the day I became more conscious of God's constant, abiding presence with me as I completed ordinary tasks and enjoyed relationships as a part of everyday life.

Spiritual Practice: Lectio Divina

Lectio Divina, or Sacred Reading, is a way of listening to God through Scripture, alone or in community. This practice leads us to pray Scripture. Lectio Divina can be done alone during your quiet times with God. It can also be done with a group of people where one person reads the prompts, a second person reads the Scripture passage, and participants listen and respond orally or in writing (or both).

- First, choose a Scripture passage you feel drawn to, or use the verses from Matthew 11 I've provided below.
- Begin by centering your mind on God's presence within you and breathing slowly and naturally. Pray for God's presence, wisdom, and insight.
- Then use the prompts provided below before each reading of the Scripture passage. Read slowly and prayerfully, pausing for about 30 seconds after the Scripture passage has been read.
- You will either read (yourself) or listen to four readings of the same passage, each one with a different purpose. A prompt will be read slowly before each reading with a short, 30-second pause given after each reading. Read slowly, pausing often to give participants a chance to absorb the words and any personal meaning.
- After the third reading (only), journal your unedited response to God. This could be in the form of a prayer or simply jotted reflections on what God might be saying.
- After the fourth reading, simply rest in God's loving presence for a few minutes.

When doing Lectio Divina in a group, you may spend a few minutes inviting participants time to share. This is usually an especially rich, encouraging time as people share from their hearts what God has shown them or spoken to them.

Suggested Scripture For This Practice:

Matthew 11:28-30

Choose either version or alternate versions with each reading.

"Are you tired? Worn out? Burned out on religion? Come to me. Get away with me and you'll recover your life. I'll show you how to take a real rest. Walk with me and work with me—watch how I do it. Learn the unforced rhythms of grace. I won't lay anything heavy or ill-fitting on you. Keep company with me and you'll learn how to live freely and lightly."
— Matthew 11:28-30, MSG

"Come to me all who are weary and heavy-laden (burdened) and I will give you rest. Take my yoke upon you and learn from me, for I am gentle and humble in heart and you will find rest for your souls. For my yoke is easy and my burden is light.
— Matthew 11:28, NIV

Lectio Divina With Prompts

Preparation: Breathe, Center, Pray

1st Reading: Read—Read (or listen to) the Scripture passage as a whole. During this first reading, get a sense of what the passage is generally about. Pay attention to the who, what, when, where, and why of the story.

> Read the Scripture, then pause.

2nd Reading: Meditate—Read (or listen to) the Scripture a second time. Notice a word, phrase, image of God, or feeling you might be drawn to. Hold that word, phrase, image, etc. in your mind and heart. Underline it or write it on your journal page.

> Read the Scripture, then pause.

3rd Reading: Respond—During this third reading, reflect on how the word; phrase, image, or feeling seems to connect or relate to your life. How might God be speaking to you? What is His invitation to you? After reading the Scripture, journal your initial, unedited responses to God as a prayer, a question, or a wondering.

> Read the Scripture. Then allow five or six minutes for journaling and listening for what God may want to say to you.

_____

_____

_____

_____

_____

4th Reading: **Contemplate**—Read (or listen to) the Scripture a fourth time and then simply rest in God's presence. Set aside any agenda and enter into a peaceful place of experiencing God's unconditional love for you. Using your imagination, look into His face or allow yourself to be held in His embrace. Enjoy just being with Him.

> Read, one last time, then simply be with God in whatever way you choose. Relax and sense His loving presence.

Reflections On The Practice

- What word or phrase in the passage were you most drawn to? _____

- Were you able to sense God speaking a specific, personal word to you? If so, what was it? In most cases you will be drawn to a word or phrase. If you were not, simply express gratitude for the truth of God's Word and His abiding presence.

Note: Part of the mystery of this kind of prayer involves being open to noticing how God shows up for you. You may get a word or see an image or a short video, or just have a sense of Him loving you. Allow God to speak in the way He chooses. Sometimes there will only be silence. Enjoy being with Him in that silence.

- When, where, and how might you be able to make this practice more of a habit?

_____

_____

_____

_____

_____

Scripture Verses To Read, Study, Ponder, And Memorize

"Come to me, all you who are weary and burdened, and I will give you rest. Take my yoke upon you and learn from me, for I am gentle and humble in heart, and you will find rest for your souls. For my yoke is easy and my burden is light."
—Matthew 11:28-30

Be still and know that I am God.
—Psalm 46:10a, RSV

My heart is not proud, Lord, my eyes are not haughty; I do not concern myself with great matters or things too wonderful for me. But I have calmed and quieted myself, I am like a weaned child with its mother; like a weaned child I am content.
—Psalm 131:1-2

Extending The Learning

Categories Of Spiritual Practices

Engaging in spiritual disciplines or practices invites God to change us. These practices encourage us to give God access to our whole selves as we trust and surrender to Him. In essence we are saying, "*God, I can't really change myself in the ways that make me a person who loves and lives the way Your Son, Jesus, did. So, I give you permission to do your work of transformation in me. I yield myself to you as I pray, read Scripture, worship, or partake in the other spiritual practices.*" Remember, disciplines are like tools in our spiritual toolbox or well-stocked kitchen, helping us make space for God's grace to operate in our lives. They help us focus our minds, hearts, and bodies on Him.

Another way we can determine the practice that is right for us is by looking at our current personal needs. For example, maybe you desire to know God better, or you want to learn to slow down and be present to life and relationships. Maybe you need help getting free from bitterness or un forgiveness that keeps you stuck in depression.

We can also look at our desires. The following are three categories of desires. There are many more practices that could fit into the three categories, but these are a few to consider.

Category	Description	Practices in this Category
Giving Up	These are disciplines that help us surrender to God, which is an important foundation for spiritual growth. Here we let go of pride, control and self-importance. We acknowledge that Jesus is our Lord. We look at Jesus' model of submission as He took up His cross and gave His life so that we could be born anew in Him.	Submission, surrender, repentance, confession, worship, welcoming prayer, simplicity, slowing, retreat
Drawing Near	These are disciplines that help us draw close to God toward a more intimate relationship with Him. We grow and thrive spiritually out of a close friendship of daily two-way communication with Him.	Solitude, silence, prayer, meditation, waiting, listening, fasting, study, journaling, Lectio Divina, Visio Divina, Imaginative Prayer using Gospel stories, Prayer of Examen
Reaching Out	These practices help us cultivate community and connection with others. We become God's hands and feet as we partner with Him in serving and bringing His Kingdom to the world.	Service (all kinds), fellowship, mutual submission, sacrifice, witnessing, justice, spiritual direction, spiritual friendship, hospitality

Check out Adele Calhoun's *Spiritual Disciplines Handbook: Practices That Transform Us* for a much more expansive list of spiritual practices connected to our personal desires.

Nuggets For The Journey

Meditate on this simple, beautiful poem by St. Teresa of Avila called simply, "Breath."[28] Let it help you **slow down** and be in the **present moment**. **Enjoy God's company** as you sit with Him, knowing that He is in every breath you take.

Breath

*This magnificent refuge
is inside you.
Enter.
Shatter the darkness that
shrouds the doorway...
Be bold.
Be humble.
Put away the incense, and
forget the incantations
they taught you.
Ask no permission.*

*Close your eyes and
follow your breath to the
still place that flows to
the invisible path that
leads you home.*

"Ruthlessly eliminate hurry from your life."

–Dallas Willard's answer to the most important thing we can do to continue growing spiritually[29]

8 FORGIVENESS, PART 1

Opening Up A Conversation On Forgiveness

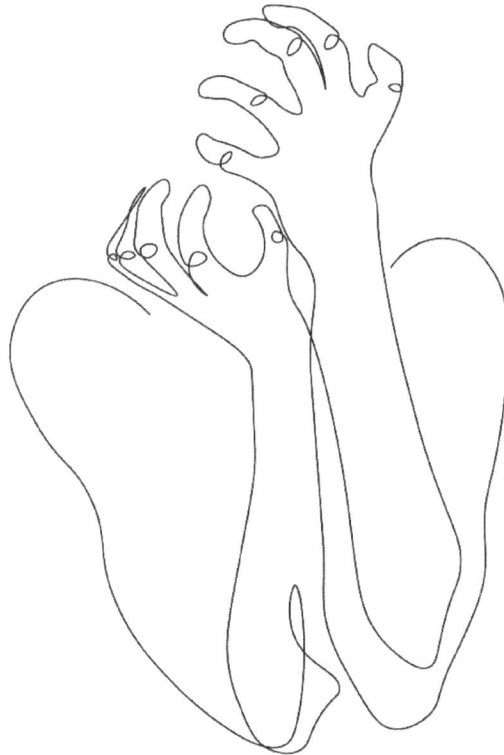

"It requires a tremendous leap of faith to imagine that your own childhood or past—punctuated with pain, loss and hurt—may, in fact, contain a gift."

—WAYNE MULLER

Night Of Rage

A sudden force of emotions startled me awake. A volcanic eruption rose from the pit of my stomach. I was inexplicably filled with an overwhelming rush of rage. The feelings were completely foreign to me. I sat straight up in bed, dismayed by the intense anger that flooded my mind like a thick blackness. It was the wee hours of the night, around 3 a.m. The rest of the family lay fast asleep. My mind was a jumble. Overwhelming, uncontrollable negative emotions tore at my heart. Desperate for relief, I gently nudged my husband awake, my thoughts and feelings spilling out.

"I feel consumed by rage, like nothing I've ever felt before. I can't go back to sleep. I don't know what to do! It's like all the pain and abuse I've ever experienced is pushing up from within me like a volcano violently erupting. I think I even hate my mother?"

Was this really me saying these words out loud? The sound of them seemed loathsome to me. I was repulsed by my own admission.

Gone was the polite, composed person I had been mere hours ago. It was as though every painful, destructive action taken against me, every demeaning word spoken to me or about me, each of which I had pushed down out of awareness, was now wildly bubbling up from within the depths of my being. As I tried to explain what was happening to me, tears of sorrow from my wounded heart made it difficult for me to speak. ElRoy and I moved to the family room where I rode my stationary bike for a few minutes, giving my emotions a chance to settle.

As we sat together on the couch I described a list of ways my mother, knowingly or unknowingly, had sabotaged me as a person. I shared flashbacks that were running through my mind like race horses rounding the track at the Kentucky Derby. Some of my wounds stemmed from abuses I had experienced during my early childhood years. Others were related to intense, ongoing feelings of rejection and betrayal even into adulthood. I had no memory of her ever hugging me or telling me she loved me. I had never experienced the gentle tenderness of a mother's caress. This current explosion of anger brought with it memories of being rebuffed and insulted by my mother, even in front of my friends.

After a period of sharing some of the most vividly painful memories, I grew calmer. Though the awareness of my emotional wounds had almost totally engulfed me in grief, I slowly began to sense an openness to God's loving presence and His forgiving nature. Yet instinctively I knew this one explosive session wouldn't solve the years of pain and neglect. How on earth could I deal with all of this and begin to receive the help and healing I so desperately needed?

My mother had once tried to explain that she, herself, "was never nurtured. So, I guess I don't have what it takes to nurture you. You may have noticed that I almost never hug anyone, but you are especially hard to hug."

What did she even mean? "Especially hard to hug?" Too stunned to process such a statement or to even speak, I had simply walked away. She had lived a tormented life. One of 15 children, she received very little personal attention from either of her parents. Childhood neglect, sexual abuse, and surviving two abusive marriages had taken their toll on her. I was grateful that night for my husband's support and kind attention as I shared the depths of my grief and feelings of betrayal.

Never having experienced a mother's nurturing love had left me with a deep sense of loss and rejection.

As we prayed together, God's love and peace washed over me like a gentle spring rain, bringing a sense of hope. The words of the psalmist rang through my mind: *"But I have calmed and quieted my soul, like a weaned child with its mother, like a weaned child is my soul within me"* (Psalm 131:2, ESV). God's Spirit and His sacred Word soothed my wounded soul.

ElRoy and I talked a while longer. When it seemed like there were no more words and my body was drained of its tears, we prayed again. I gave God access to my broken heart in the best way I knew how. I was ready to consider moving toward forgiveness. I was sure the process would be long, but I had already taken the first steps: acknowledging the offense and getting in touch with my deep-rooted feelings of rejection. I would need help and support to navigate the rough waters of grief, letting go, and healing from the pain. Through the weeks and months ahead, I would have to be focused and intentional. As for now, I was exhausted from the night's traumatic battle. Thankfully, I was able to fall fast asleep.

Learning To Conceal Destructive Negative Emotions

Negative emotions, especially anger, have an uncanny way of exploding. We become masters at concealing or stuffing our feelings far below the conscious level. The pain we don't want to feel is out of sight and out of mind—until it resurfaces, often at the most unwanted times.

As a church-going person, I learned many things about the types of behavior and emotions that were most desirable for Christians. As a first-born child, I was already inclined toward perfectionism, always striving to please my parents, other authority figures, and especially God. My bed was made every day. I didn't talk back. Being six years older than my nearest sibling, I became the reliable, responsible family babysitter. I developed a good girl persona because it was expected. Most of the time I displayed characteristics that others found highly acceptable. Any negative or inappropriate qualities were carefully tucked away and pushed down below the surface. I made sincere attempts to pray and read God's word every day, taking life and my spirituality seriously. While reading and studying the Bible for life direction, certain verses stuck out to me, like this one: *"Get rid of all bitterness, **rage, anger**, harsh words, and slander, as well as all types of evil behavior"* (Ephesians 4:31, NLT). Noticing that rage and anger were linked together with "all types of evil behavior. I became averse to expressing negative emotions, including anger and rage. Though I wasn't conscious of it, a subtle core of anger was developing deep within me, which I continued to push down into my subconscious mind.

There seemed to be no place for rage, anger, or bitterness in my life, so I obediently kept them at bay. Suppressed. Never to be spoken of. I was not always consciously aware of these unacceptable, well-controlled emotions. As a child in Sunday School, I was taught to forgive those who offended me. Wanting approval for my "good" behavior I often responded to insults, negative comments, or boundary breaches with carefully prescribed polite statements, such as, "I know you didn't mean it" or "I still love you" or "It's okay, I forgive you." Assuming I was doing the right thing, I smothered my offender with niceties and simply pushed the pain away from my conscious experience, dutifully countering evil with good.

This was very confusing, since I had witnessed so much anger from the adults in my family. My alcoholic father often spewed biting curse words, harsh and demeaning accusations, and engaged in physical abuse to keep all of us, including my mother, in line. One of my earliest childhood memories was witnessing my father chasing my mother around the house, threatening her with a sharp kitchen knife. Frozen stiff with fear, my eight-year-old-self watched as he cornered her in the living room. She was trapped. There was nothing either of us could do. Unexpectedly, he turned. With the knife held tightly in his hand he cut down a decorative Christmas bell that hung from the ceiling, somewhat satisfying his rage. As a child, I never knew when or why these frequent explosions of rage would erupt.

A few years later, after my mother had divorced my father, she remarried. A similar pattern of abuse continued. One day during dinner, my stepfather, displeased with the meal my mother had prepared, threw his plate of food on the floor. Then he ravaged the kitchen, pulling food out of the fridge and throwing it on the floor. As if that wasn't enough, he proceeded to drag dishes out of the cupboard, letting them crash in pieces at her feet. "Clean up this mess!" he yelled. We kids stood helplessly watching. Somehow, I worked up the courage to speak out in protection of my mother. As I walked toward him, sputtering something about Mom doing the best she could, he pushed me as hard against the kitchen wall. I fell to the floor, stunned and helpless to save her from his angry outburst.

It was early morning a few years later. I tried hopelessly to start my old beater of a Rambler, so I could get to school. It just wouldn't start! I ran inside to my stepfather for help. Unfortunately, his efforts to start the car also failed.

"What did you do to this car?" he asked accusingly.

"Nothing!" I shot back.

"You must have done something!" he yelled. "It started yesterday!"

"I did nothing!" I retorted.

Before I could even see what was happening, he slung his fist into my face, giving me a black eye. I don't remember what happened after that. I do know he told me to get into his car so he could drive me to school. Mortified by what had just happened and embarrassed by my black eye, I asked him to drop me off a half block away from the school so I could collect my thoughts and so no one would see him. I was so embarrassed.

Neither my father nor my stepfather professed to be Christians. Rarely had either of them darkened a church door. My mother, however, took my younger siblings and me to church each week. For me as a young Christian woman, expectations seemed higher than they were for men. Anger, rage, and bitterness were taboo. Trending in my family were the phrases "Speak only when spoken to" and "If you don't have something nice to say, don't say anything at all." My negative self-talk looked something like this:

> Anger and rage = Bad.
>
> Therefore, angry Beverly = Bad.
>
> The absence of anger or rage, only forgiveness = Good,
>
> Therefore, Beverly, saying only kind words and forgiving others = Good.

Expressing a different point of view, disagreeing with a responsible adult, or challenging my parents was not acceptable.

I didn't fully understand what forgiveness was or why it was so important. I did consider it my Christian duty, necessary for maintaining my squeaky-clean image and staying out of trouble. It wasn't until many years later that I learned that there is something so much deeper that happens when we fully experience God's grace toward us and begin to let go of our feelings of bitterness. It is when this happens and we lean into His healing that we experience forgiveness.

What Is Forgiveness, Really?

I find it helpful to think of forgiveness as a process of letting go of anger, bitterness, or resentment toward someone who hurts or offends me, whether intentionally or unintentionally. This is not the same as saying the abuse or the event are okay.

> *What we are forgiving is* **not the act—not the violence, the incest, the neglect, the offense, the divorce, or the abuse.** *We are forgiving the actors, the people who could not manage to honor and cherish their own children, their own spouse, or their own life in a loving gentle way.*
> —Wayne Muller[30]

Forgiveness is primarily for our benefit, because it frees us to live our lives unburdened by the negative emotions that can bind us to the past and steal our joy in the present. Forgiveness allows us to free ourselves from the control of the person who hurt us.

In order to understand forgiveness more fully, we need to understand what it is not. Prayerfully read through the statements below and **check** the ones you most often struggle with or that might be a problem as you try to move forward with the process of forgiveness.

What Forgiveness Is Not:

- A requirement to relate to that other person in the future
- The same as trusting
- Approving of another person's behavior
- Saying the offense against you wasn't all that important
- Ceasing to be appalled at what happened to you
- Forgetting the offense
- Believing it is okay with God that the offense happened
- Believing you shouldn't tell the other person how angry you are
- Believing the unforgiveness will resolve itself over time
- Saying that the offense wasn't painful, or that it doesn't still hurt
- Waiting until the person says they're sorry
- Believing you are unimportant or that your personal boundaries don't matter[31]

If you checked any of the above statements, prayerfully bring them to God. Ask Him to bring enlightenment and wisdom as you consider developing healthier boundaries.

A Word On Developing Healthy Boundaries

Developing and maintaining healthy boundaries is an important skill to have in our toolboxes. Healthy boundaries help us set limits around our physical, emotional, financial, and digital spaces. Boundaries are essential, but setting them does not always come naturally. Most of us have to work at both establishing and maintaining them. Here are some important things to remember when establishing boundaries:

1. Boundaries help us determine where and how much we are open to sharing certain aspects of our lives.

2. Boundaries help us define our identities, bring order to our lives, preserve our purpose and mission, and protect us from violators.

3. Boundaries help increase our self-esteem and self-respect.

4. Boundaries should be communicated as clearly, calmly, and respectfully as possible.

5. Boundaries are a requirement for honest, direct communication.

The Destructive Effects Of Unforgiveness

Forgiveness is important because the alternative—holding onto bitterness—affects our mental, emotional, spiritual, and physical health. **Though the hurts that result from the offense are painful, we intensify the pain when we allow it to fester and continue for days, months, or even years. When this happens, our spiritual growth becomes stunted.**

Health professionals say that unforgiveness, anger, bitterness, resentment, and other negative emotions are most likely stored in various parts of our body, our cells and our organs. These stored emotions affect us on many levels, though we may not realize this is happening. Negative emotions can also affect our immune systems, leaving us vulnerable to a variety of illnesses, such as chronic anxiety and even cancer. Unforgiveness can also cause us to mistrust and isolate ourselves from others. But there is hope.

Forgiveness sets us free. It allows us to experience life more fully, to continue to grow and develop spiritually and emotionally. Forgiveness supports the body's natural immune response. Unforgiveness not only affects our relationship with the offender, but it also affects our relationships with friends, family members, and even with God and ourselves. Forgiveness frees us to trust again, to develop and enjoy the beauty of healthy relationships. It's important to understand that it may not be wise to trust the offender. We need to discern whether that person is trustworthy. Then we can learn to set healthy boundaries for ourselves.

Questions To Ponder, Journal, Or Discuss

Many of us have experienced painful experiences that left us struggling with bouts of depression, anxiety, low self-esteem, and occasional disturbing flashbacks. We might have felt ourselves lacking the resilience to recover easily. If you are in a safe place and feel able to, search your heart and mind for moments of childhood trauma that may still sting when you think of them. These traumatic experiences may be opportunities for forgiveness. Trauma can include major abuse (such as molestation, beatings, physical harm, etc., as well as lesser, but chronic abuses such as name calling, neglect, unreasonable demands, boundary issues, etc.

1. Does anything specific come to mind for you as you review childhood memories? Are there situations from your teenage years or even adulthood that cause emotional pain and anguish?

2. Are there people you'd like to forgive or wish you knew how to forgive? What feelings, emotions, or thoughts stop you from walking in the freedom that forgiveness can bring?

3. Are you aware of any past or present thought patterns that have kept you stuck, unable to move toward spiritual and emotional growth?

_____

_____

_____

_____

_____

_____

_____

_____

As you continue reading this chapter, my prayer is that you will be able to access the gifts of

God's forgiveness, healing, and wholeness, and that these gifts will make a difference in your life going forward. Even if you just *begin* a conversation with God about forgiveness, God can meet you right where you are and walk the distance with you. Will you open your heart to the glorious opportunity to be free from resentment and bitterness? Will you trust God to love and nurture your heart and soul through the process? He is faithful and He is good.

What Prevents Us From Forgiving?

I found that it was important to see through my false beliefs and embrace the truth of what forgiveness was and was not. Because they become so embedded in our everyday belief systems, many people don't fully understand that we carry around false beliefs. However, this is an important prerequisite in the process of forgiveness. False beliefs about forgiveness can keep us trapped and unable to move into freedom.

Hindrances To Forgiveness That Block Us

When we have been betrayed, devalued, rejected, or harmed in some way, Satan, the enemy of our souls, can use pain and unforgiveness to block our growth. Knowing this, why wouldn't we be jumping up and down to be first in line to forgive the person who offended us? What is holding us back? Take a look at the following four hindrances to forgiveness. As you read, consider which of the four may be getting in the way of your ability to forgive.

Hindrance #1 - We think we have forgiven everyone we know but haven't, because we have an inaccurate or incomplete understanding of what forgiveness is and is not.

Hindrance #2 - We do not see the signs of bitterness or anger in our lives, so we believe we are free from unforgiveness. They remain hidden in our subconscious because to admit or accept them would mean we are bad. Our predisposition and aversion toward shame and guilt keep us in denial.

Hindrance #3 - We don't realize or believe what the lack of forgiveness has done in our lives, how it has and continues to harm us.

Many people repeatedly go through the list of offenses against them, ruminating on the pain and staying stuck. This allows negative messages to continue dominating their thoughts. When we ruminate on the past, the negative messages become an increasingly big parts of our daily reality. After we determine what the negative messages are and we have grieved them well, we need to replace them with true messages. This will allow us to see ourselves as God sees us, not as we were unjustly named or labeled in the past.

We tend to repeat these negative statements in our minds, which further carves them into our neuroplastic brain. What messages from the past do you continue to ruminate on? What negative beliefs do you carry with you? Add them to your journal. Name them to tame them. If left unchecked, these past negative statements can continue to haunt you your whole life. The following are some examples of negative messages. Do any of them apply to you? Perhaps you can think of some of your own.

- "My alcoholic father humiliated me. I felt worthless."
- "Kids at school picked on me for being the smallest in the class."
- "My teachers were hard on me and never appreciated my efforts."

- "I was a loner and had very few friends. I wasn't well-liked."
- "My wife/husband left me. I felt unloved and unwanted."
- "My friend betrayed me. I wasn't worth protecting."
- "No one ever really listens to me or respects my opinion."
- "My mother always/never…"

Write your own negative messages in your journal, if any come to mind.

_____

_____

_____

_____

_____

When we relive or ruminate on old offenses, we give tremendous power to the other person or situation we are fixated on. It is as though we are handing a knife to that person, inviting him or her to touch our wounded spot and hurt us again and again. Once you've listed a few false beliefs of your own, reframe them to be more positive. Give your neuropathways a change to reprogram your automatic thoughts into something more helpful.

For example, "Kids at school picked on me for being smallest in the class" could become:

"Good things come in small packages" or "Greatness from small beginnings."[32]

You get the idea.

Hindrance #4 - We believe we have a good reason not to forgive.

We may think the severity of the offense or the role of the offender needs to be addressed before we can forgive, but forgiveness is not based on what the offender has done. Forgiveness is something between us and God that allows us to freely live and move into a life of wholeness and healing.

Prayerfully consider whether any of these hindrances are keeping you from accessing freedom through forgiveness. If so, bring your thoughts and concerns to God or share with someone who can support you on the pathway to forgiveness.

Scripture Passages To Read, Memorize, Or Meditate On

Choose one or two of the verses on forgiveness below or find one yourself. Read it several times. Read slowly, meditating on the words and listening for a specific word or phrase that carries weight. Do you sense a message from God? You may also want to memorize a verse as you progress through your forgiveness process. Memorizing and rereading Scripture helps move the words from our mind to our heart, where it changes us more easily. What word or phrase in the verses below are you most drawn to?

But you are a forgiving God, gracious and compassionate, slow to anger and abounding

in love. Therefore, you did not desert them.
—*Nehemiah 9:17b*

Be kind and compassionate to one another, forgiving each other, just as in Christ God forgave you.
—*Ephesians 4:32*

And when you stand praying, if you hold anything against anyone, forgive them so that your Father in heaven may forgive you your sins.
—*Mark 11:25*

For if you forgive other people when they sin against you, your heavenly Father will also forgive you. But if you do not forgive others their sins, your (heavenly) Father will not forgive your sins.
—*Matthew 6:14-15*

Jesus said, "Father, forgive them, for they do not know what they are doing."
—*Luke 23:34*

Effort Is Required - Doing The Work

Over the period of about six months, I carefully searched my heart and my memory for negative and traumatic events from my past. I read two books on forgiveness and began working methodically through the process outlined in a workbook on forgiveness. One by one, I focused on each person in my past that had been a source of childhood pain. I took my time, thoughtfully and thoroughly grieving each major event or person responsible. I purposefully paid attention to how I may have contributed to the problem myself. I offered forgiveness not only to those responsible but also, where appropriate, to myself for my part.

I also offered forgiveness to God, because at times I blamed Him for allowing bad things to happen. I spent one month on each person as God brought them to my mind. I wanted no stone left unturned.

With each person or situation, I worked through my barriers to forgiveness and my misunderstanding about what forgiveness really was. I also faced and dealt with the hindrances that kept me bound. I wanted forgiveness to be real, not contrived. Parts of the process were painful as I relived the discomfort and trauma I had endured. Some parts were exhilarating as I learned to experience honest, heartfelt forgiveness and let go of bitterness.

This following story is an example of a memory from my early years of marriage. In it I had to work through forgiving myself, my husband and God.

Pain can often lead to greater maturity, because we tend to grow through the things we suffer.

Mourning To Dancing: Surprised By Joy

I was surprised to find myself pregnant, since we'd only been married a couple of months. Actually, I hadn't really wanted children. I was an elementary school teacher with 31 new fourth-grade students each year, which was at times exhausting, and seemed quite enough for me to handle. On the other hand, ElRoy, wanted 12 children. This precipitated many unsettling discussions during our first year of marriage.

The first six months of pregnancy, happily, went by without a hitch. My mom had helped me decorate the nursery. Together, we found a dark blue gingham fabric patterned with tiny pink rosebuds, a design that would work for either a boy or a girl. She skillfully trimmed the crib bumper, sheets, and pillows with off-white eyelet fabric. Everything seemed perfect for our new arrival and I was actually getting excited. My hair appeared shinier, and my skin glowed more brightly. Pregnancy seemed to look good on me. I enjoyed feeling the baby's subtle movements and the tiny tummy kicks. Motherhood was beginning to feel like a very special blessing.

During Lamaze class, ElRoy and I met a beautiful young medical student. As a part of her college nursing class, Lisa was required to partner with a couple through their pregnancy experience. We volunteered to invite her along on our journey. During the next few months of preparing for the birth, and then in the initial stages of caring for our new baby, Lisa would be by my side, helping me and learning right along with me. Her long, curly blond hair shone like sunlight, prompting me to call her my angel. We became fast friends. With Lisa's support my life seemed a little brighter and more hopeful.

A month later, my labor pains finally began coming harder and faster. It was time to go. ElRoy and I met Lisa at the hospital as the nervous excitement of birthing a baby for the first time began to build. Not knowing the gender of the baby, we had picked out a boy's name, Matthew, and a girl's name, Stephanie, after one of my best friends. Early on, ElRoy and Lisa were such a big help, rubbing my back to calm my nerves and encouraging me to breathe slowly. At one point my blood pressure began skyrocketing, and the doctor announced the dreaded word, CESAREAN, as a possibility. The doctor tasked ElRoy with getting on the proper clothes and gear so he could be a part of the birthing process.

Shortly after changing and re-entering my hospital room, ElRoy became faint and had to leave the room to regain his balance. Thankfully, he returned in time for the birth.

After five hours of labor, it was time to push. It didn't take much effort. The baby easily slid out and into the doctor's hands. "It's a girl!" he announced. But my baby didn't make a sound. Where was the burst of energetic crying, so familiar after a birth? "It must be twins," the doctor reported. "This baby is too small to have filled all that space." Before I had time to question what might be going on, the nurse quickly wrapped Stephanie in a blanket and showed me her beautiful, tiny round face. She was adorable; so sweet and rosy-cheeked. Then I heard someone say, "We need to take her upstairs, immediately, for further testing. Someone will be with you shortly with the results." Little else was said. *"What?"* I wondered, astonished. *"Why wasn't I allowed to hold her, for even a few minutes?"* The excitement of the night morphed into exhaustion and confusion. There was no second baby. Something was very wrong. ElRoy, Lisa, and I were left alone, a puddle of dread and disorientation in the sterile hospital room.

During the long-drawn-out hours, ElRoy knelt beside me, holding my hand and praying. We spoke very little as we waited in the fearful unknowing. Lisa stood close beside me and began to audibly pray.

A while later, the doctor returned to inform us that our daughter, Stephanie, had a genetic disorder: 18 trisomy syndrome. This meant that she had an extra chromosome 18 in most of the cells in her body.

"Her organs have not developed correctly," he said. "Her hands and feet are webbed, and she weighs only about three pounds. She had to go immediately on life supports and be placed in an incubator. You will be able to see her in the morning."

The doctor's words left me in a hollow state of shock. He informed us that he and the hospital psychologist would be there in the morning to talk with us and help us understand our options. Everything was a blur. No wonder they hadn't let me hold her. It was impossible to process all that had just happened. My hopes were dashed as I sank into a state of depression. Both ElRoy and I were physically and emotionally exhausted as the nurse wheeled me to my room for the night. As visiting hours drew to a close, ElRoy and I prayed together, and then he left. I sank yet deeper into despair. My excitement and hopes for our little family had been stripped away. I held onto God in the only way I know how, and to a tiny thread of hope that this nightmare was only a passing dream.

In the morning ElRoy returned just as the doctor arrived to explain the hard cold facts of the diagnosis.

"Most 18 Trisomy babies are never even born alive. Of those that are, only about 13 percent live past a week, and almost none survive past a year. You have two options. Option one: Stephanie would need approximately 12 to 15 surgeries in order to function without life support. Even then, she would survive only as a vegetable, unable to do anything for herself. Her esophagus is connected to her lungs, which means she can't eat without a feeding tube. Your other option is to allow us to take her off life support completely and let her go. She will suffocate to death, unable to breathe on her own."

Waves of depression and exhaustion swept over me. How could this be happening? What should we do? Both options seemed unacceptable.

After the doctor left, the psychologist came to offer us coping strategies. My mind was numb and my emotions dull as I tried to listen to her words of encouragement.

"You will want to hold Stephanie and tell her how much you love her and how precious she is. This will be an important part of the grieving process. Try to wait six months before trying to get pregnant again. Otherwise, you'll just be filling the void left by Stephanie. Your body and your emotions need recovery time."

A while later, the nurse on duty took us to the nursery to visit Stephanie for the first time. We were given a private room in which to be with her. She was hooked up to several monitors, with a blanket wrapped around her. The nurse handed me her tiny, swaddled body. As the psychologist had encouraged us to do, we held her. Through tears of grief, we told her how much we loved and enjoyed holding her. It did us both good. She was our beautiful little girl, and we wanted her to feel all the love we could shower upon her. I desperately wanted to wake up from this traumatic dream. The thought of making a decision regarding the life of our first-born child, our beautiful daughter, brought both of us to tears again.

The more I held Stephanie, the more I loved her. What an impossible choice we had in front of us. I couldn't imagine having the tubes removed and letting her die. But I also couldn't bear the thought of allowing her to live as a vegetable. I struggled to believe I had the strength to care full-time for a child who needed that level of support. The pain of this decision was excruciating, and the sorrow seemed too much to bear. ElRoy and I prayed for hope and discernment tearfully clinging to each other.

Over the next couple of days, we continued to hold Stephanie and whisper words of love and encouragement to her as often as we could.

That evening after dinner, as visiting hours began, friends and family members arrived, a few at a time. Within 30 minutes, my entire room was filled with so many people that I, honestly, don't think another person could have squeezed in. I was overwhelmed by the display of support being offered in the form of balloons, flowers, prayers, cards, gifts and loving kindness. Together, we prayed and sang songs of hope and faith. Then, as visiting hours drew to a close, our visitors began leaving, until only ElRoy remained.

ElRoy had been serving on the elder board of our church. Coincidentally, they were scheduled to meet that very evening, so he planned to bring our difficult decision to the group. He left with a promise to confer with our friends on the elder board for additional wisdom, and to return as soon as he could the following morning. Alone, in despair and exhausted, I fell fast asleep.

When ElRoy arrived the following morning, he reported that his time talking with the elders had been helpful. One of the elders had gotten a beautiful vision of Stephanie as a young girl, dancing at the feet of Jesus. After a time of prayer, several of the elders shared with ElRoy that since the chances of her living for more than a week were very slim, and even then, her quality of life would be quite poor, we should probably have the tubes removed and let nature take its course. Jesus would be waiting for her and would be able to make her whole. Both the vision and the supportive words brought peace to our hearts. We could not have done this without the encouragement and support of our friends. That afternoon we let the doctor know what we had decided. We knew Stephanie would soon be in a better place, where she would be healed and could dance freely.

Wanting to assure Stephanie of our love for her, we visited her one last time. We held her, telling her that she would soon see Jesus, and that there were dancing shoes waiting for her in heaven. Saying goodbye was solemn and tearful. It was the last time I saw her alive.

Once home, we were told to wait for the hospital to call and let us know when Stephanie had taken her last breath. Four days later when the phone rang, I somehow knew it was the hospital. A friend who was visiting picked up the phone and handed it to me. Stephanie was no longer with us on this earth. I cried tears of grief.

"Blessed are those who mourn, for they will be comforted."
—Matthew 5:4

As a family and church community, we began to organize a "celebration of life" service for Stephanie. Many who had supported us through the ordeal volunteered to speak. Through this process something unexplainable, yet undeniable, began happening inside of me. In my grief I turned to God, as I had been doing, but with even more desperation. Feeling such pain, I could do nothing else but cling to Him. Over the next few days, God's presence began to feel more real, more tangible. The comfort of His embrace was palpable, and I pressed into Him through the pain. It was as though a seed of joy had been planted in my heart and was growing stronger. As sorrow and grief began to melt away, this seed of joy burst into complete *joy of the Lord* within me. It didn't make rational sense. In some supernatural and unexpected way, God had bestowed upon me a gift. My soul felt like dancing.

> *You turned my wailing into dancing; you removed my sackcloth and clothed me with joy.*
> —*Psalms 30:11*

What a beautiful treasure my heart was holding. Many years later, I wondered if, in some supernatural way, my soul was connected to Stephanie's, and God was allowing me to sense her joyfully dancing at Jesus' feet. I treasured this thought in my heart and often visualized her dancing beautifully, wearing her new red dancing shoes.

Questions To Consider And Journal

- When have you been overcome with grief or sadness? Journal about one of those times here.
- What kinds of loss have you suffered? It might have been the loss of a person close to you. It could have been the loss of something you held dear, such as a job, a dream, your reputation, or something more tangible. Write about your experience and the feelings that accompanied that loss.
- Were you able to process those feelings with a friend, a counselor or someone you trust? If not, you may want to plan a time to share with someone safe.

Scripture References To Ponder, Memorize Or Meditate On

> *Then he broke through and transformed all my wailing into a whirling dance of ecstatic praise.*
> —*Psalms 30:11 (TPT)*

> *I will turn their mourning into gladness; I will give them comfort and joy instead of*

sorrow.
—Jeremiah 31:13b

*There is a time for everything, and a season for every activity under heaven…a time to weep and a time to laugh, a time to mourn and a **time to dance**.*
—Ecclesiastes 3:1 and 4

Note: *You may have endured a great loss or suffered ongoing wounding as a child. This may have included being spoken to gruffly, or being told you were stupid, a liar, or worthless. The phrase, "What's wrong with you?" or worse may have been spoken over you. You may have witnessed or been the victim of physical or sexual abuse. Pay attention to how these things affected you and the feelings you are left with as the result.*

As I progressed through each step of the forgiveness process, I was able to work through to more spiritual and emotional freedom—more joy, and more acceptance of the inconsistencies and imperfections of others and even my own. I grew in my ability to trust in God's unconditional, compassionate, healing love for me. Gratitude for this path to greater wholeness welled up within me. It was exciting to see real results in my personal life: more peace of mind came from an inner experiential-knowing of God's loving, healing, forgiving presence with me.

Though I had learned quite a bit about the healing process, I wanted to continue becoming the kind of person who could more easily let go of anger and bitterness on a daily basis. I wanted to keep walking in my newly-acquired greater freedom.

Letting go of our pain and sorrow can't be rushed into or hurried. Real, transformative work takes time. For many of us, forgiveness is a process that occurs after a long thoughtful look at our heart's desire to be more whole, and for our character to be more like Jesus'.

But you are a forgiving God, gracious and compassionate; slow to anger and abounding in love.
—Nehemiah 9:17b

We have opened up a conversation on forgiveness, which has laid the groundwork in preparation for us to actually engage in the practice of forgiveness. For some, forgiveness may come more easily, and for others it may take more time.

This slow work of God can't be rushed.

Try to honestly tune in to your thoughts and emotions as we end this chapter.

- Do you have a desire to forgive those who have harmed you?

- Do you long for the freedom that comes as you let go of past hurts, bitterness, and unforgiveness? It is for our own sake that we let go and forgive.

- If you are not ready, you may want to review chapter 7 at another time.

- If you are ready, you may want to pray this prayer as we begin the next chapter, where we will engage in the practice of forgiveness:

"Lord, Please Help Me Become More And More The Kind Of Person Who Can Forgive Easily And Often. Amen."

Now, if you're ready, let's begin.

9 FORGIVENESS, PART 2

Engaging In The Practice Of Forgiveness

"To forgive is the highest, most beautiful form of love. In return, you will receive untold peace and happiness."

—ROBERT MULLER

Waves Of Healing

It had been nearly six months since beginning my forgiveness journey. This may seem like a long time. For others, it may seem like not nearly long enough. For some, this journey may take a lifetime. It is the slow work of God that brings true transformation. Each of our pathways toward healing through forgiveness will be unique.

It seemed important to mark the completion of my process, which had been so meaningful and life-changing for me. I was learning to be the kind of person who could forgive more easily and freely. That part of me seemed to be becoming more like Jesus.

> *But you are a forgiving God, gracious and compassionate, slow to anger and abounding in love.*
> *—Nehemiah 9:17b*

I began to bring closure to my forgiveness process by writing individual prayers of forgiveness and collecting a small rock for each of my offenders. I had spent approximately a month each to thoroughly process every person and situation. In quite a dramatic way, God had led me to this moment. He had helped me work through the emotional night of rage and given me a desire to be free from the bitterness I hadn't even realized I was carrying. Once I understood the depth of my anger and how it was personally affecting me, I wanted the forgiveness to be real, lasting, and transformative. Of course, much of the letting go had happened already as I worked through the process. Now, I was delighted to celebrate my growth and freedom by making a public statement of forgiving and letting go, with God's help and blessing.

On a clear summer day, I drove to my favorite beach in Del Mar. Holding my small bag of rocks and neatly folded prayers, I stood on a cliff at Powerhouse Park. As I stood, overlooking the calm aqua-blue Pacific Ocean about 100 feet below me, I prayed. One by one I read my prewritten, heartfelt prayers and threw a rock as far out into the water as possible. Rhythmic waves seemed to wash away any residual unwanted painful emotions as I watched from high above the water. I said goodbye to the pain that had held me captive for so long, and to the unforgiving attitude I had held against each person. Cool coastal breezes gently blew over me. My soul felt grounded and free.

Savoring the beauty of this special moment I stood still, in awe as I let go and drank in God's healing love. The scene in front of me was breathtaking. My soul soared with thanksgiving. I felt clean and whole. I remembered Jesus' words in Mark 11:25:

> *"And when you stand praying, if you hold anything against anyone, forgive them, so that your Father in heaven may forgive you your sins."*

A lifetime of grief had been lifted from my heart over the past six months. In its place was gratitude for the deep work of healing that had occurred. A closer, more intimate relationship with God had gently infused me. A calm confidence quieted my soul as I drove home.

I felt like a new person, wrapped in God's generous grace. Within me, all was well. The words of Julian of Norwich floated through my mind:

All shall be well, and all shall be well, and all manner of thing shall be well.[33]

Cultivating A Forgiving Heart

Forgiveness isn't just something we do. It's a way of being. It is not a one-and-done task. It's about becoming the kind of person who forgives easily in the natural flow of life. During the six-month process of doing the work, I was cultivating a heart that longs to forgive and the freedom that comes with it: freedom from bitterness, anger, and carrying a grudge.

Forgiveness starts from an awareness of God's loving presence, and an experiential-knowledge that God is good, and that He is for us. Embracing the knowledge that God has good intentions toward us invites us to open ourselves to the healing work of forgiveness and letting go of past hurts. God's loving presence becomes a safe place from which we can honestly explore our woundedness without feeling guilt or shame. He longs to forgive us as a gift of His grace. He walks arm in arm with us and restores us to Himself. Imagine that kind of love: accepting us as we are, in spite of what we've done, and leading us by the hand into wholeness.

As stated earlier, it's helpful to enlist the support of a trusted friend, spiritual director, counselor, mentor, or other professional who can also help provide a safe place of support as we walk through the process of forgiveness. When I first began this journey, my husband and my spiritual director provided comfort and encouragement. I was so fortunate to have their calm acceptance and wisdom. Authors who wrote on the topic of forgiveness also helped provide a structured plan for my forgiveness journey.

Once we are grounded in God's love and have the support needed, we can start the process by acknowledging painfully abusive situations as well as their accompanying emotions. Then we will be ready to grieve the losses we've experienced. My encouragement is that you take your time as you name the abuses and the associated negative feelings. Write them down in your journal or on the worksheet provided further along in this chapter.

> *Hurry is the enemy of your spiritual life.*

Move through each step of the process thoughtfully and thoroughly. Ask God to give you guidance to know when and how to move to the next stage of the journey. Though this chapter may take longer to move through than some of the others, if forgiveness is something you need in your life, it will be well worth the time.

Spiritual Practice: Self-Examination

Engaging in honest Self-Examination will prepare you for the practice of forgiveness.

Find a comfortable place to sit that is free from distraction. Begin to focus on your breathing, taking slow deliberate breaths. Journal your thoughts and the prayers of your heart related to the questions and concepts below.

- From your comfortable chair, imagine yourself in a 'safe place', where you are surrounded by the love of God, free from worry or distraction. This can be a real or imaginary spot. My safe place often involves a beach scene, since that's where I feel almost an instantaneous connection with God. Where might your unique, safe place be? Notice the sights, smells, and sounds of this very special place where you will enter into a conversation with God. Visualize yourself as He sees you through His eyes of loving compassion and kindness. Ask God for His help in allowing you to see yourself through His welcoming grace.

- Begin a dialogue with God/Jesus regarding something that may have come up today or recently related to forgiveness or unforgiveness.

- At what stage do you find yourself in the process? Check any that apply.
  - Acknowledging an offense
  - Getting in touch with the related feelings
  - Grieving the offense
  - Wanting to let it go
  - Feeling resistance
  - Having frozen feelings
  - Wanting to forgive
  - Wanting to heal
  - Wanting to deny the pain

- Engage in a conversation with God about where you are and what you desire from Him. Talk to Him as openly as you would with an intimate Friend.

_____

_____

_____

_____

_____

_____

_____

_____

- Perhaps you sense the need to begin thinking about people or events in your past that caused you pain or are currently causing you pain. Do you desire the freedom that comes from letting go and forgiving the offender, or are you not yet ready?

- Are you thinking of way too many excuses for NOT forgiving? Where are you in this process? Be as honest as you can.
- Maybe you are grateful for God's redeeming, healing work in your life thus far.
- Journal your responses to some of the questions above as a prayer.

_____

_____

_____

_____

_____

- Do you desire a spiritual friend, mentor, or spiritual director to support you? Would you like to call or text someone and ask for prayer as you engage with God on this intimate matter?
- Ask God's Spirit to guide you as you move forward in beginning to forgive.
- Pay attention to the condition of your soul. Begin the forgiveness process where you can and in the way you can.

Preparation: Readiness For Forgiveness

My hope for you is that you will desire to experience the kind of life change that comes from honestly forgiving, from your heart, those who have harmed you through either abuse or neglect. Now that we've seen the benefits of forgiveness as well as the things that hold us back, you may be ready to begin taking steps toward forgiveness.

Forgiveness Often Takes Time And Space For Our Hearts To Be Open And Ready. That's Why The Preparation Stage Of This Process Is So Important. It Allows The Work To Go Deeper And, Therefore, Become More Lasting.

Close your eyes and go back to your "safe place"; the one you created in the exercise above. Begin by imagining yourself sitting in that beautiful very personal "safe place" with Jesus. Breathe slowly and deeply as you notice the scene that is becoming your beautifully inviting "safe place." Are you indoors or out in nature? Use all of your senses to imagine what you might see, hear, and smell. Take your time. What kind of day is it? What textures and tastes are available for you to enjoy? Where is Jesus in relationship to you? If you desire, draw a little closer to Him, remembering that His intentions toward you are good and His love is immense. As you honestly open your heart to Him, the power that sets you free is available, right now. Spend time sharing your hopes and dreams for a more fulfilling life. Center or ground your thoughts and emotions in the knowledge that He is right beside you all the way.

With Jesus as your guide, take an inventory of the painful memories in your life that still keep you bound up and un-free. Share these with Jesus as you would share with an intimate friend.

Then begin the process of forgiveness using the steps outlined below. Read through all of the steps in advance to get an idea of what the process is like. Then use the **"Steps to Forgiveness Worksheet"** to guide you.

Note: There is no need to hurry this process. Time, intention, and self-compassion are needed to make this a truly transformative process.

Steps To Forgiveness

Note: These Steps to Forgiveness were developed by Robert McGee.[34] The commentary is my own.

1. **Make a list.** List some painful memories from your childhood, and the people or particular situations that brought you great sadness or harm.

2. **Choose a memory.** Pray and ask God to help you choose a memory or a person from your list. You may wish to choose one person, but list several painful memories related to that one person. Describe the situation in as much detail as you can on the **Steps to Forgiveness Worksheet** or in your journal. When I worked through my forgiveness process, I used the Forgiveness Journal below with some tweaks of my own. I made copies for each distinct painful memory and each person I wanted to forgive. You may choose to do the same.

3. **Acknowledge the pain.** Get in touch with the pain, loss, or suffering you experienced. Name the feelings/emotions as clearly as possible. Avoid trite words like *bad*, *sad*, or *mad*. Instead use more descriptive words such as *belittled*, *demeaned*, *betrayed*, etc.

4. **Notice your feelings and grieve the losses you felt.** Sit with them, noticing the depth of your feelings and the negative messages they brought, messages like "I am unlovable," "I am defective," or "I am invisible." This step may take a while and require some time for grieving in order to move to the next step.

5. **Begin to let go.** Say goodbye to the pain. If the offender is someone you will probably never see again, say goodbye to the person who caused the pain. Let it/them go. Use your imagination to help you see the person in your mind as you visualize saying goodbye. Lean into God's compassionate love for help and support. You might want to imagine yourself placing the person and/or the painful memories in Jesus' hands. If you have gotten in touch with a negative label spoken against you, you may want to replace it with the truth. For example, "I am defective" could be replaced with, "I am complete in Him."

6. **Notice any areas of resistance.** Are you aware of any hardening of your heart, fear, or hatred? If so, ask God to soften your heart. It might be helpful to imagine handing the pain and the person to Jesus. The charts "What Forgiveness is Not" and "Hindrances to Forgiveness that Block Us" (in the previous chapter) can be helpful. Name the hindrance. This step is important, because it helps us see the ways we are tricked by false thinking. Then let go of the pain and the offending person.

7. **Invite in healing and forgiveness.** Pray, *"God make me the kind of person who easily forgives. Holy Spirit, help me receive this grace of forgiveness as a gift from you."* Acknowledge the truth that Jesus' death and resurrection have settled the issue of our

forgiveness already. *"He [God] rescued us from the domain of darkness and transferred us to the kingdom of His beloved Son, in whom we have redemption, the forgiveness of sin"* (Colossians 1:13 and 14, NASB). We have been delivered and freed from the penalty of sin because Jesus paid our ransom with His death. 2 Corinthians 5:14 (NASB) states, *"For the love of Christ controls us, having concluded that this one died for all. Therefore, all have died."* Jesus died as the substitute for our sins. His death brought about our redemption and forgiveness once and for all. Forgiveness has already been accomplished; past, present, and future. Confess any known sins and receive the free gift of forgiveness.

8. **Write a prayer of forgiveness.** When we are able to forgive, we are more aligned with the character of Christ. Jesus forgave his accusers. *"Jesus said, 'Father, forgive them, for they do not know what they are doing'"* (Luke 23:34). You may want to acknowledge that it is God who enables you to forgive through the power of the Holy Spirit. Ask Jesus to give you the words as you pray your prayer of forgiveness. Write this prayer in your journal. You may want to keep your prayers available in case you want to use them to bring closure to the process. Some people burn them. I chose to throw my prayers into the Pacific Ocean, watching the waves carry away any traces of unforgiveness. It was a glorious celebration of my freedom.

9. **Express gratitude.** Thank God for His gracious free gift of forgiveness and the freedom it brings.

Repeat these steps as often as needed with the same person, or with as many people or offenses as you need to gain freedom. Use the **Steps to Forgiveness Worksheet** on the following page. You might want to make copies of this page so you can reuse it for different people or to deepen the process with the same person. I duplicated this and used it during my six-month in-depth work on learning to forgive. Before I began, I made copies for each person I wanted to forgive, and additional copies for specific situations that had caused me intense lingering pain. You might prefer to copy each of the headings in your personal journal and work through the process there. Starting with #2 on the Steps to Forgiveness Worksheet, as you repeat this process as many times as you need to with different situations or people.

Steps To Forgiveness Worksheet

Note: These Steps to Forgiveness were developed by Robert S McGee, Searching for Peace, Merritt Island, FL: Search Resources, 2003. The commentary is mine.

1. List several painful or traumatic situations or people from your past. This list should include people and situations that carry a heavy negative weight in your mind. Some of these may have come to mind in some of the earlier chapters.

_____

_____

_____

_____

_____

_____

_____

_____

_____

2. Prayerfully choose which person, situation, or memory you will focus on today. Describe the event and the primary person/s involved.

_____

_____

_____

_____

_____

3. Get in touch with the pain. Describe and sit with your feelings for a while. (Don't rush this.)

_____

_____

_____

_____

4. Name any deeper negative feelings or messages brought on by the person or event. Take time to grieve your pain and losses.

_____

_____

_____

_____

_____

5. If you're ready, begin to let go. Say goodbye to the pain and the person who caused it (if they are no longer a part of your life). Replace negative labels or messages with positive ones.

_____

_____

_____

_____

6. Notice any resistance. Name the resistance or hindrance that may be keeping you from forgiving.

_____

_____

_____

_____

7. Invite in healing and forgiveness.

_____

_____

_____

_____

8. Write a prayer of forgiveness.

_____

_____

_____

_____

_____

9. Express gratitude to God for partnering with you in this process and helping you forgive the offender.

_____

_____

_____

_____

Reflection On The Practice Of Forgiveness

Forgiveness can bring with it positive changes in feelings and attitudes toward the offender. You may notice a shift in your emotions or in the intensity of the pain. Your level of resentment or need for vengeance may decrease.

Over time, the practice will become easier and more natural. Like learning to ride a bike or drive a car, our first attempts can feel awkward or laborious. If practiced regularly, forgiveness will eventually become a joy as you experience your relationship with God, others, and yourself being restored, and your heart being set free.

- Which parts of the practice seemed easy and which parts seemed more challenging?
- Did you notice any areas of resistance as you worked through the process? If so, how would you describe your feelings?
- How might this practice help you move toward greater freedom and love?
- How did God meet you through this process?

_____

_____

_____

_____

This is not a one and done kind of thing. There are probably more people and more situations that will warrant the use of the Steps to Forgiveness Worksheet. You may find it helpful to make several copies of the worksheet, so that you can continue using the strategies you've just experienced.

Note: If you don't feel ready to continue this practice, continue reading and ask God to open your heart to the desire to be free from anger, guilt, shame or resistance. Listen for his still small voice and the Holy Spirit's guidance as you move forward.

Extending The Learning: Continuing The Process

Kudos if you have worked through this chapter and put some or all of the suggestions to good use! This can be an intense chapter for those who intentionally and honestly delve into past offenses and work through to forgiveness. Being authentic with yourself is a part of growing in intimacy with God.

I encourage you to continue this practice throughout your life. It's an important aspect of continued healing and transformation into Christlikeness. Forgiveness helps free us from feelings of guilt and shame that often plague us as we reflect on experiences like abuse, defamation of character, or betrayal. Engaging in the practice of forgiveness helps us answer Jesus' invitation to be set free from the bitterness, anger, and hatred that can block the light of His beautiful presence. It's about continually living in the freedom and wholeness of His healing love.

During this process you may have noticed that who you really need to forgive is **yourself.** This is very common for some of us who tend to be harder on ourselves than on others. Learn to be kind to yourself as you work through painful experiences. You may think you could have done more or that you could have done something better than you did. Learn to give yourself grace. God certainly does. Forgive yourself. On the other hand, if you did hurt someone, intentionally or unintentionally, ask for forgiveness; make amends.

There also may be times when you have to forgive God. When ElRoy and I were working through our grief over the loss of our first daughter, Stephanie, we both had to come to grips with waves of blaming God for allowing this to happen. Fortunately, our relationship with God was strong enough that we were able to withstand brief moments of doubt and discouragement that led to anger. Thankfully, we had each other and our church family to help us.

One person we may also need to forgive is *ourselves*. If God has already forgiven us, why shouldn't we?

Learn to be kind to yourself on this Journey toward wholeness.

But what happens if we don't or can't forgive someone?

Consequences Of Not Forgiving

Mental health professionals are quick to tell us that holding onto bitterness, resentment, or anger can affect us negatively in many ways. Not forgiving:
- inhibits our ability to cope with or resolve the issue

- keeps us stuck in the past
- can inhibit the natural function of our immune system
- leads to us reliving offenses over and over in self-inflicted emotional re-injury
- can cause us to offend others due to our reaction to our past offenses
- blinds us to God's forgiveness of us
- torments our souls with an underlying stress, anxiety, or perpetual conflict
- can cause us to become angry with God
- can lead to a sense of alienation or isolation from others and from God
- can cause us to resist God and to lack trust in Him and His grace
- can lead to suffering from an impaired ability to give and receive love, the result of harbored anger, hatred, or bitterness
- can lead to us attempting to control others.

Questions will undoubtedly arise as we continue to practice forgiveness. Below are some additional thoughts that I found helpful as I and others have dealt with unforgiveness.

Nuggets For The Journey

Doubt:

For some of us, forgiveness can be confusing. We can go through all of the steps and feel great about our progress, but then days, weeks, or even months later we become weighed down with questions and uneasiness about the validity or the finality of the process. We might ask ourselves questions like: *"Was this real?"* or *"Is there more I have to do?"* or *"If I still feel the hurt and pain, did it work?"* or *"Did I actually forgive my brother? I'm not sure?"* It's important to revisit God's Word for the truth. When we openly and honestly come before God with a humble and contrite heart, the Bible says, He hears us. We have the assurance that the work is done.

> *The Lord is close to the brokenhearted and saves those who are crushed in spirit.*
> —*Psalm 34:18*

He already knows our heart and our intentions. He sees our desire to forgive, be forgiven, and be set free. Scripture says,

> *If we confess our sins to God, He can always be trusted to forgive us and take our sins away.*
> —*I John 1:9 (CVE)*

It is finished! Done! If we authentically ask for forgiveness from a heart of repentance (meaning to turn around and change), it is accomplished!

Though God has forgiven us and we have forgiven our offender, the memory of the pain may reappear, and we may begin to obsess over it. This can be an opening that allows bitterness or anger to creep back into our hearts. When that's the case, I find it helpful to be honest with God about negative feelings and ask Him to take those feelings from me. Remember, He wants only what is for our good. His desire for us is to walk in love, joy, and freedom, not weighed down with doubts about His love for us, or caught in the jaws of anger and bitterness.

You may wonder: "**Did I really forgive_____?**"

Questions like this one may continue to arise until you learn to fully accept God's once and for all forgiveness.

I experienced many questions along the way as I worked through the process of forgiving key people in my life. Something that I found helpful was to revisit or reaffirm my act of forgiving and being forgiven. For a period of time I kept six small quartz hearts on my dresser. Whenever I passed by my dresser, I placed my hand on the hearts and expressed gratitude to God for His forgiveness and for helping me forgive those who offended me. I prayed a simple prayer. The following are some examples:

"Lord, I receive your forgiveness. Thank you for giving me a heart that forgives more and more easily."

"Lord, thank you for helping me forgive _____. Sometimes the memory of the offense causes me to resent _____. I give this resentment to you, and I receive your forgiveness. Please give me a clean heart toward you."

Touching the quartz hearts reaffirmed the previous work of forgiveness, allowing me to access it anew. Having the physical representation (the hearts) of my act of forgiveness, and being able to rest my hand upon the rocks seemed to affirm the reality of the completed work. Forgiveness really had occurred!

Allow God to reaffirm or remind you that He has forgiven you once and for all!

Visualization

Use your imagination to visualize yourself being gently held by a caring Abba Father, or being hidden under His nurturing wing, or resting within His compassionate heart. This can provide powerful healing images, and help us develop new neural pathways of belief. These visual images enable us to lean into and experience the truth of His forgiveness and nurturing love.

He heals the brokenhearted and binds up their wounds.
—Psalm 147:3

Like a mother hen, "He will cover you with his feathers, and under His wings you may take refuge; His faithfulness will be your shield and rampart.
—Psalms 91:4

Through this type of visualization, Jesus invites us to access intimacy with Him as we draw closer. Spend a few minutes meditating on these verses and see God loving you. Try to imagine yourself crawling into the heart of God and resting there, trusting in His faithful promises to you.

Gratitude

Expressing a heart of gratitude can lift our spirits and redirect our thoughts from the offender to images of our loving heavenly Father. Redirecting our thinking helps create positive thought patterns. As these positive thoughts are revisited and repeated, they can become more firmly implanted in our minds, easily accessed when the stresses and anxieties of life threaten to flood us.

> *Filling our hearts with praise, gratitude, and worship opens the door of access to God's healing grace in our lives.*

May you sense God's warm smile upon you as you continue your journey toward becoming the kind of person who forgives easily and who experiences the gifts of His forgiveness and freedom.

I have found that each time I forgive someone, I experience increasing depth and intimacy in my relationship with Jesus.

Some of the concepts from this chapter have been gleaned from:

Wayne Muller, *Legacy of the Heart: The Spiritual Advantages of a Painful Childhood* (New York: A Fireside Book Published by Simon and Schuster, 1992).

Robert S McGee, *Searching for Peace* (Merritt Island, FL: Search Resources, 2003).

10 LIVING OUR BEST LIFE WITH INTENTION

Creating A Life-Giving Rhythm

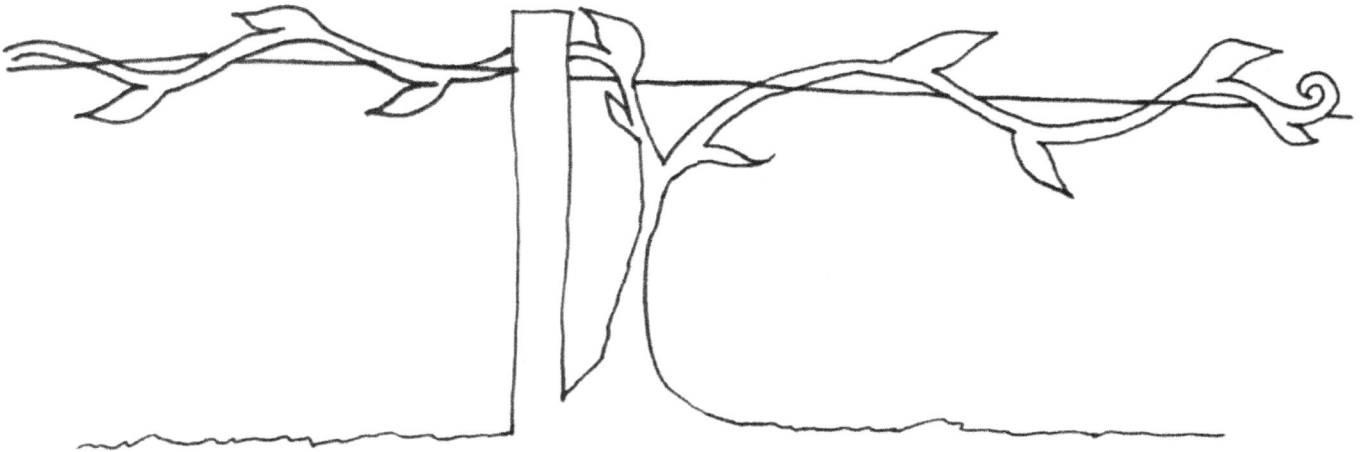

"We long to see our lives whole, to know that they matter. We wonder whether our many activities might ever come together in a way of life that is good for ourselves and others. Lacking a vision of a life-giving way of life, we turn from one task to another, doing as well as we can but increasingly uncertain about what doing things well would look like. We yearn for a deeper understanding of how to order human life in accord with what is true and good."

—CRAIG DYKSTRA AND DOROTHY BASS, *PRACTICING OUR FAITH*

Pilgrimage To Ireland

As we entered the hot, dry Ocotillo Desert in Southern California, I breathed a sigh of relief, knowing that we would have a couple of days of rest, refreshment, and spiritual retreat. We'd been coming to this desert home for the past 10 years. It was the second home of our friends, Ann and Butch in Canebrake Canyon. The ocotillo plants, desert animals, and miles and miles of sand and rock presented a beautifully rugged backdrop to our drive. Sometimes we visited the desert home alone as a couple. At other times, we joined Ann and Butch, engaging in meaningful conversations, the entertaining card game Chicken Foot, and generous amounts of quiet time to ponder what God might be up to in our lives.

We were mostly silent during the two-hour drive in January of 2015. My heart was heavy with sadness and frustration. It had been an emotionally tough week. ElRoy and I seemed to be on different wavelengths, reacting to each other more than usual. Swirling in my head were so many troubling questions. Why did our communication periodically spiral downward? Why did those pesky childhood issues resurface so often, causing us to misunderstand and pull away from each other? Would this weekend offer a fresh perspective and lift my dampened spirits? Pulling up to the desert home, my mind was ablaze with wonderings. I felt desperately hopeful.

After an almost silent drive, we had arrived. Our friends greeted us on the back porch and welcomed us in. Once unpacked, the guys went out back to work on a construction project—building a guest house. Ann invited me to join her on a visual Celtic pilgrimage through Ireland via DVD. Sitting on pillow-laden chairs and drinking tall glasses of ice water, we were transported to a far-away land across the sea.

The pilgrimage was led by author, poet, speaker, and Catholic priest John O'Donohue. His heart-warming, winsome approach to Ireland's coastal area was replete with descriptions of monstrously high cliffs and bleak rocky terrain surrounded by the churning Atlantic Ocean. By contrast, there were lovely, serene scenes of velvet-green landscapes meeting still blue waters.

In my imagination I was swept away to that magical isle. Waves of joy and refreshment settled in my soul throughout the hour-long video pilgrimage. I was amazed that I could experience such a richness of beauty by simply watching images on a video recording. I was surprised to feel I really had been transported to a different location. The visual enjoyment of Ireland's of lush green landscape against a soft blue sky, and glistening deep blue ocean were dream-like and invigorating. My soul and spirit were lifted.

I had gone on several in-person pilgrimages, mostly in Europe, which had been life-changing. It was surprising that our video experience was almost as engaging and inspirational—minus the cost and the 17-hour flight. In my journal I wrote the following words:

> *Beautiful poetry, paired with glorious, majestic Irish coastal vistas, infused with God images; delighting my senses. I shed sweet tears of release. For the first time that week, my tears were those of comfort, rather than pain. Silently, I breathed a sigh of relief, releasing the sadness and sorrow, and welcoming a heart of gratitude.*

The video had vividly displayed glimpses of pristine, coastal vistas of Ireland. The beauty of God's creation had brought me to a place of grounded calm. John O'Donohue had poetically described the timeless majesty of Irish history and terrain. I felt both humbled and at peace in the deep places of my soul.

> *When I consider Your heavens, the work of Your fingers, the moon and the stars, which*
> *You have set in place, what is mankind that you are mindful of them?*
> *—Psalm 8:3-4a*

So rich and profound was my experience that I repeated the entire video pilgrimage by myself the following day, revisiting and absorbing the beauty of dramatic cliffs, sandy beaches, and grassy knolls.

Before we knew it, our two-day mini retreat had come to an end. As we drove down the gravel road away from the desert home, we admired the ocotillo plants in full bloom, showing off their brilliant orange-red flowers and the plump barrel cacti topped with chartreuse flowers. Together my husband and I recounted the many ways God had met us and encouraged our hearts. We chatted easily all the way home.

What a difference this short but sweet mini retreat had made!

Spiritual Practice: Revisiting

On day two of our mini retreat, all alone, I had replayed the DVD and revisited the inspiring pilgrimage scenes in order to reignite my soul's sense of connection to God. I was engaging in a practice called "revisiting". I often find this practice helpful, because as I replay or reimagine a powerful scene, a passage of Scripture, or a meaningful event, it encourages me to answer God's invitation to allow him to touch my heart and soul at a deeper level. With each repetition, the meaning or message is absorbed at a deeper level, and the truth is embedded more securely in the soul.

Use your imagination to enter into the Scripture below. Intentionally revisit that same Scripture on several days this week, allowing God to make it more and more personal to you. These words of the psalmist reflect a beautiful delight in God Himself.

Pause and meditate.

After reading the Scripture two or three times through, try to picture the scene before you.

> *As a deer pants for streams of water, so my soul pants for you, my God.*
> *—Psalm 42:1*

> *I long to drink of you, O God, drinking deeply from the streams of pleasure flowing from*
> *your presence. My longings overwhelm me for more of you!*
> *—Psalm 42:1, TPT*

- Were you able to visualize the scene in your imagination?

- What did you notice?
- Were you able to sense a closeness to God?
- What might make the experience more meaningful for you?
- Would doing a practice like this out in nature be helpful?

Your personal practice of revisiting might focus on a nature scene, a verse or passage from Scripture, a stimulating passage from a book, a heartfelt worship experience, a painting, a sculpture, inspiring poetry, etc. My experience of God's presence seems to expand and deepen when I repeatedly relive a meaningful past experience. I am drawn to a more intimate place with Him. Eventually, I come to simply enjoy being with Him as His beloved daughter, and I delight in Him.

Choose #1, #2, or #3 (There's no need to do them all, unless you want to.) **to engage in the spiritual practice of Revisiting.** This can be a powerful exercise, especially if you are able to see where God may have present in the memory. Lines for journaling are at the end of #3.

Revisiting #1: Try This Yourself - Revisit A Place Of Natural Beauty

1. Look through an album of pictures from a previous vacation, or find a video online showing vivid scenes from a place of importance you have previously visited. This could be a place that brings great pleasure and delight as you think back on it and remember specific highlights.

2. Jot down some notes regarding your past visit, highlighting what made that place memorable.

3. Close your eyes and place yourself in the scene again, as you remember it. Enjoy being surrounded by the beauty and significance of that place once again. Try to enter in with all of your senses. Notice what you saw, heard, smelled, touched, or tasted.

4. Let the knowledge of Jesus' presence and love surround you as you sit quietly with him.

Revisiting #2: Revisit Something Of Spiritual Significance

1. Think of a time/Scripture/event where you experienced God speaking to you, or especially enjoyed being present with Him and close to His heart.

2. If you have the verse, journal entry, etc. readily available, reflect on it again.

3. Jot down what made this so eventful or meaningful.

4. Close your eyes and ask God to continue to speak to you through this previously significant event, Scripture, etc.

5. Consider its personal meaning for you as you lean into the presence of God. What might God want to say to you?

Revisiting #3: Revisiting A Childhood Memory

1. Name some childhood and/or adult memories that bring you joy.

2. Pick one memory that seems most vivid.

3. What qualities of your experience make it especially meaningful or memorable? Are there any patterns you see as you think through why you were so deeply touched by a certain event, movie, Scripture, etc.?

4. What response does this activity elicit within you?

5. How might you use the practice of revisiting to enliven your spiritual life?

Spiritual Practice: Creating A Life-Giving Rhythm Of Life

Have you ever wondered if it is possible to live each day knowing you are in a loving relationship with God, constantly aware of this as you live out your calling in God's kingdom and the world at large?

Having a "rule of life" or a "rhythm of life" (interchangeable terms) allows us to clarify our deepest values, most precious relationships, most genuine hopes and dreams, most meaningful work, and highest priorities. It allows us to live with intention and purpose each day, in the present moment. More importantly, it allows us to live in constant relationship with God, experiencing His loving presence through the ups and downs and twists and turns of the events and relationships of each day.

Practically speaking, a rule or rhythm of life helps us consistently and intentionally organize our life around what matters most. It is a group of activities and practices that guide us to a deeper fuller life with God, others and ourselves.

When we hear the phrase "rule of life," it can be off-putting. We might imagine a list of dos and don'ts, or rules that we would be bound to follow. For most of us, this doesn't feel inviting. A rule of life is not equivalent to creating a list of rules to follow.

The word "rule" derives from the Latin word *regula*, which refers to a way of *regulating* and *regularizing* our lives so that we can stay on the path we have set for ourselves. I like to think of a rule of life as a trellis that offers support for a plant, helping it to grow in a certain direction. A rule or rhythm of life helps us articulate our intentions and identify the ways in which we want to live. When we fall short of these intentions, we can revisit that rule; and it will show us how **we can return to the path we set for ourselves and recapture our original vision.** It is not fixed and rigid, but it can and should be adapted to our season of life and our present circumstances, shaped to fit our current needs and desires. Because the word "rule" can be troublesome or unappealing, you may prefer to use the term "rhythm of life." For some of us, "rhythm" has a more fluid, inviting connotation. Ruth Barton uses this term in her book on spiritual practices, *Sacred Rhythms: Arranging our lives for Spiritual Transformation.*[35] I recommend this book for gaining a deeper understanding of the concept of a rule/rhythm of life.

The rule of life was first developed in the third and fourth centuries as a part of the monastic tradition of the church, when Christian monastic communities first came into being in the deserts of Egypt. Even though rules of life were originally developed for communities, they can also be useful for individuals. Through creating a rule of life, an individual can put into words the things that he or she values most, enabling them to identify ways in which they can be achieved or lived. Here is an example of a Rule of Life.

Sample Rule Of Life

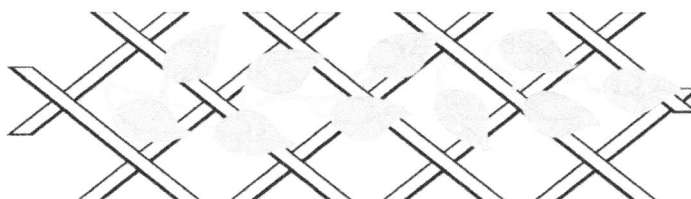

Daily

Physical exercise

Choose <u>one to three</u> from the following to do each day:

- Scripture reading
- Lectio Divina/imaginative prayer/meditative reading
- Prayer
- Journaling/reflection
- Gratitude journal
- Devotional reading

Weekly
- Study Scripture
- Prayer of Examen
- Family time
- Worship in community
- Simplify
- Professional growth
- Specific area of service

Monthly
- Silence/solitude/quiet morning
- Relationship: small group (community)
- Area of service

Quarterly
- Quiet day/private retreat
- Training/professional growth

Yearly/Seasonally
- Structured retreat
- Pilgrimage (every few years)

Now let's look at some guiding principles for developing your own rule or rhythm of life:

A rule of life is first about SUBTRACTION, then about ADDITION.

Let's Face It, Many Of Us Are Stressed, Worried And Fearful.

The process of creating a rule of life can feel overwhelming. Most folks add too many activities into their rule of life in an effort to do this practice well. It's easy to overload on more practices than we need or can handle. Consider deleting some of the activities that currently take up space in your life, but are not helpful or life-giving in accessing more of God's presence. For example, viewing less TV or listening to fewer podcasts can free up time for something more life-giving. Eliminating some of the mindless scrolling on social media could give you more quality time and space for God. Believe me, I know this can be challenging. However, the benefits are well worth the effort. There were times in my life when God seemed to be encouraging me to even say no to additional church commitments, especially with my propensity toward too much doing, people-pleasing, and achieving.

Living out your rule of life should be joy-producing. You might be in the habit of checking your phone in the morning, scrolling on Facebook, or checking the news, but you have very little time to commune with God or to simply rest. To be honest, this has been a temptation for me. I have begun setting my phone far out of reach before bedtime, and not scrolling or listening to content right before bed. My mornings and evenings now seem more peaceful and positive.

Your rule of life should allow time for rest and recuperation. Taking a short rest or nap can actually provide more energy to complete tasks and goals than if you hadn't taken that needed break. If you find yourself exhausted day after day, it's a pretty good sign that you may need to allow yourself space for rest or sleep.

A rule of life is not static. It is an organic, ever-changing process.

Developing a rhythm or way of life based on spiritual practices takes time. You will need to manipulate this rhythm as you would a piece of clay, molding it into what is most workable and beneficial for you. Over time as your needs change, your rhythm of life will also change and adapt to a new season.

When I first began developing a rule of life as a younger Christian, my use of spiritual practices mostly centered on Bible reading, Bible study and prayer. These were the practices I was most comfortable with at the time, and they had sustained me spiritually.

Over time I began incorporating practices such as meditation, Prayer of Examen, pilgrimage, and prayer walks in nature. I didn't stop using my original practices, I simply sprinkled in a few others as I learned them and found that they addressed a specific need or desire. I didn't do all of them every day. I spread them out as needed or as the opportunity (e.g. the chance to go on a pilgrimage) became available.

An effective rhythm of life will be very personal and unique to you.

Out of His divine love, God created each of us *uniquely* in His image. Each of us is a one-of-a-kind masterpiece designed for a beautiful purpose in His kingdom on earth. Living out our own unique rule of life can help align us to that purpose. It reflects our particular goals and priorities. It takes into account our areas of weakness and strengths. Our highest calling and our most precious personal values will help determine the content of our rule of life. Following this rule of life can enable us to achieve our most sought after hopes and dreams.

We can choose practices that address our personal areas of need, neglect, or negative patterns. For example, if we struggle with emotions such as anxiety, worry, or fear, it might be helpful to focus on practices like contemplative prayer, Scripture meditation, or the Prayer of Examen.

On the other hand, if we are plagued with depression or joylessness, practices such as celebration, corporate or individual worship, or service to others may lift our spirits and bring greater joy and fulfillment into our lives.

An effective rhythm of spiritual practices will incorporate a balance among the disciplines or practices that *come easily* to us and those that *stretch us*.

We can also choose disciplines that most naturally help us connect to God. In the previous chapter I mentioned Gary Thomas's book *Spiritual Pathways.* You can access the quiz on-line to determine your three strongest spiritual pathways among the following: *Naturalist, Sensate, Traditionalist, Activist, Ascetic, Caregiver, Enthusiast, Contemplative,* and *Intellectual.* This will help guide you to practices that will be most effective for your spiritual growth. Remember to choose practices you naturally lean toward, as well as practices that spur you on toward growth and maturity.

Our rhythm of spiritual practices also needs to be ruthlessly realistic in view of our stage of life.

There have been seasons in my life when I was blessed with an abundance of free time, but there have also been seasons with almost no white space or margin. When I was raising two small children, my only free time seemed to come late at night, when I was too exhausted to do much more than flop down onto my mattress and hope for a good night's sleep. Rocking my sweet babies to sleep became a time of prayer and worship, which provided encouragement and life-giving moments to break up my daily routine. Those quiet moments provided times to express gratitude as well as nurture for my child.

Learning new spiritual practices and incorporating them into a rhythm of life can bring vibrancy to your days. You'll also want to retain some of your most treasured "already mastered" practices. My desire for you is that you expand your vision of living where you are aware of God's loving, abiding presence in every moment of your day. As you grow in attunement with yourself and your specific needs, and as you learn which activities and practices most easily draw you closer to God's love in any given moment, you will experience greater peace, joy, and fulfillment.

Paying Attention To Your Heart's Desires

Ask God to show you what it is that your soul most longs for. Sometimes I find myself so caught up in the needs of others that I forget to stop and take a "soul stroll," looking within to see what my specific needs might be. As you ponder these thoughts, consider what you desire more in your life right now. Do you need more time with friends or family, more down time, more intimacy with God, or more time for art and creativity? What do you long for in this season, and what might that look like?

When I was a young mother of two small children with almost no time to myself, I longed for a night off—a date night with ElRoy. Once in a while family members would gift us a few hours of time together as a couple, so we could relax, regroup, and just enjoy our relationship. Having even a once-a-month date night gave us the opportunity to breathe new life into our marriage, as well as our personal lives. Now that I am no longer raising children, my needs and desires have changed. I find that I still need margin in my life; it just looks different these days. I find that I need retreat days or pilgrimages, even mini-retreat days. A half day at the beach with my journal can help provide the spaciousness that nourishes my soul and recalibrates my mind with a sense of God's nearness and the assurance of my identity in Him, as His beloved.

Take some time for a personal "soul stroll" to discern what you need these days. Then make a list of the things you desire most at this time.

1.   4.
2.   5.
3.   6.

Take Time To Listen To Your Heart

What spiritual practices have been life-giving or have produced life change in you?

_____

_____

_____

_____

_____

Are you discovering and using practices that more readily draw you into God's loving presence?

Since nature has always been one of my strongest pathways, even a five-minute break to gaze out my kitchen window at the green grass, made even more lush-looking by recent spring rain, refreshes my soul. *Noticing* the sound of the rustling of leaves as they are being jostled by a strong wind whistling through the trees reminds me of God's power and provision. Watching a hummingbird dance almost weightlessly above my head fills my mind and heart with gladness.

Practices that include nature as a pathway to God may include prayer walks through a park, or retreats in a beautiful outdoor location, where one can notice beauty as you sit or walk along a path. You may also bring nature inside—flowers, a fountain, nature sounds, or a creation-themed painting. These can be placed in a special spot where you have your personal time with God.

What are your strongest spiritual pathways, and how can you incorporate them into your rhythm of days, weeks, months, and even years?

Determine Areas Of Spiritual Need Or Weakness

Busyness causes many of us to ignore hidden wounds and blind spots. Our need to feel needed, productive, or helpful can lead us to deny ourselves the luxury of margin or white space in our lives. We absolutely need margin to be healthy and whole; space to be unstructured and moments to simply wait in God's presence for His still small voice.

Our souls crave time and space to slow down and enjoy an informal conversation with a friend or family member, to be completely present to gaze into the eyes of the person we're listening to. When this happens, we notice the joy and fulfillment it brings us, as well as them. So often I find that our greatest need is margin or space to appreciate and enjoy the person we're with, the event we're engaged in, the simple and delicious meal that's in front of us. Gratitude, appreciation, and slowly savoring foster joy within.

Practices and activities that help us slow down can include slowing, solitude, sabbath-keeping, meditation, retreat, noticing, savoring a sunset or a ____ (you fill in the blank.), slowly savoring a great meal, and expressing gratitude.

Develop A Flexible Plan

When developing a rhythm of life, think in terms of a general plan that includes practices you would like to include. What things are absolutely essential for your spiritual, emotional, mental, and physical growth? You may first want to determine the non-negotiables. Then, add others as you become more aware of how much time is available, and how many practices are comfortable and life-giving for you. Your goal is to be able to enjoy the process and the practices.

Starting small and going slowly is almost always best.

Next, think in terms of a daily, weekly, monthly, yearly/seasonal plan. Below are a few examples. You will, of course, want to choose your own set of practices. These can change over time, since the rule of life is organic and based on your season of life.

Daily: Having daily time for intentional focus on God is essential. That might include time reading God's Word, praying (as a two-way conversation with God), meditation, and discerning or listening for what God might be saying to you or prompting you to do.

Weekly: Walks through a park, on the beach, or near a pond can refresh your soul. Connections with close friends, family members, and your church family can provide community and fresh perspectives on life issues.

Monthly: Gathering together with like-minded people—friends, small groups, a spiritual director, counselor, etc.—is important for providing encouragement, guidance, and support in times of need. Journeying with others, in community, along the path toward spiritual health and wholeness is part of God's plan for wholeness.

Yearly/Seasonally: Attending some type of spiritual retreat where you can slow your pace of life, enjoy God's creation, and take a deeper and more thoughtful look at God and your walk with Him is crucial to spiritual growth. Every few years you might benefit from going on a spiritual pilgrimage. Pilgrimages have been some of the most spiritually impactful times in my life. God has met me there in profoundly beautiful and uniquely unforgettable ways.

Revise And Rework The Plan

Massage and manipulate the elements of your rhythm of life over the next days and weeks. Try some new practices the same way you would experiment with updates to your wardrobe. Pay attention to the results, both positive and negative, as you determine which practices are right for you at this time. As life situations and seasons change, continue revising and updating your rule of life until you're comfortable with the rhythm you've developed. Remember, this should be realistic for where you are on your spiritual journey. The examples and worksheet pages that follow should help guide you in this process.

Begin Simply By Considering Four Areas

As you consider each area, you may notice that one or more of them already seems strong or well accounted for. If that's the case, you may not need to add or change anything. There may be an area or two that do need special attention. Take a personal inventory of how life seems for you right now in each of the four areas. Cross off or add practices where you might like to see changes. For additional ideas, check the three lists of practices/disciplines in **Chapter 7: The Purpose of the Practices**. Remember to start small. Add one to three items to what you're already doing. You also might consider deleting things from your life that are no longer helpful to make room for what will be even more life-giving.

Consider the list of possibilities in the quadrants below to include in your four areas. Finally, you will find a **Rule of Life Worksheet** that you can use to create your personal rule of life.

Areas To Consider As You Create Your Rule Of Life:

Prayer and Bible	Rest and Refreshment
• Bible Reading/Study • Lectio Divina • Imaginative Meditation • Prayer of Examen • Journaling • Devotional Reading • Reflection • Conversational Prayer	• Sabbath • Simplicity • Play/Recreation • Silence and Solitude • Contemplation • Retreat • Breath Prayer • Care for the Body
Work and Activity	Relationships
• Service • Ministry • Exercise • Classes • Professional Work	• Emotional Health (counseling, etc.) • Spiritual Direction • Mentoring • Family • Friendship

The suggestions above are options. Gauging which practices and activities are most helpful is a very personal choice. Your decisions should be based on your season of life, energy level, areas of weakness, needs, and desires. Let what is most life-giving be part of your measuring stick for if, when, and how often you engage in a specific practice. Guard against the stress and overwhelm caused by attempting to choose too many practices. Remember the "easy yoke" if you are new at this or tend to be a perfectionist. Do include prayer, Bible reading, and reflecting daily, even if for only a few minutes. Sometimes less is more, if done with an open, seeking heart.

Your Personal Rule Of Life Worksheet

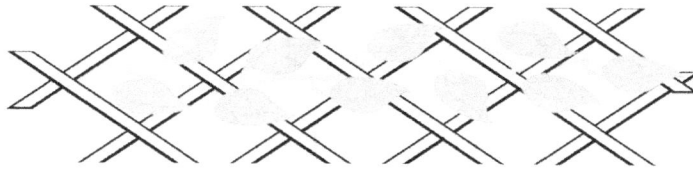

Select practices that fit into your daily, weekly, monthly, and yearly rhythm.

Daily
Weekly
Monthly
Quarterly
Yearly/Seasonally

Continuing The Learning: The Ongoing Process

When you're ready to update or revise your rule of life, which is expected as life situations and seasons change, use the questions in Appendix B (in the back of the book) on the **Living Intentionally Survey** to guide you. They will help you fine-tune your rhythm to better fit your current needs and desires.

Nuggets for the Journey

"Trust, the Highest Prayer" By Julian of Norwich

Then the way we often pray came into my mind and how, through lack of knowing and understanding of the ways of love, we make use of intercessions.

Then I saw truly that it gives more praise to God and more delight if we pray steadfast in love, trusting His goodness, clinging to Him by grace, than if we ask for everything our thoughts can name.

All our petitions fall short of God and are too small to be worthy of Him, and His goodness encompasses all that we can think to ask.

The best prayer is to rest in the goodness of God, knowing that that goodness can reach right down to our lowest depths of need.

—From Robert Llewelyn, ed., Enfolded in Love: Daily Readings with Julian of Norwich (London: Darton, Longman and Todd Ltd, 2004)

11 AWE AND WONDER

We Were Created For Joy!

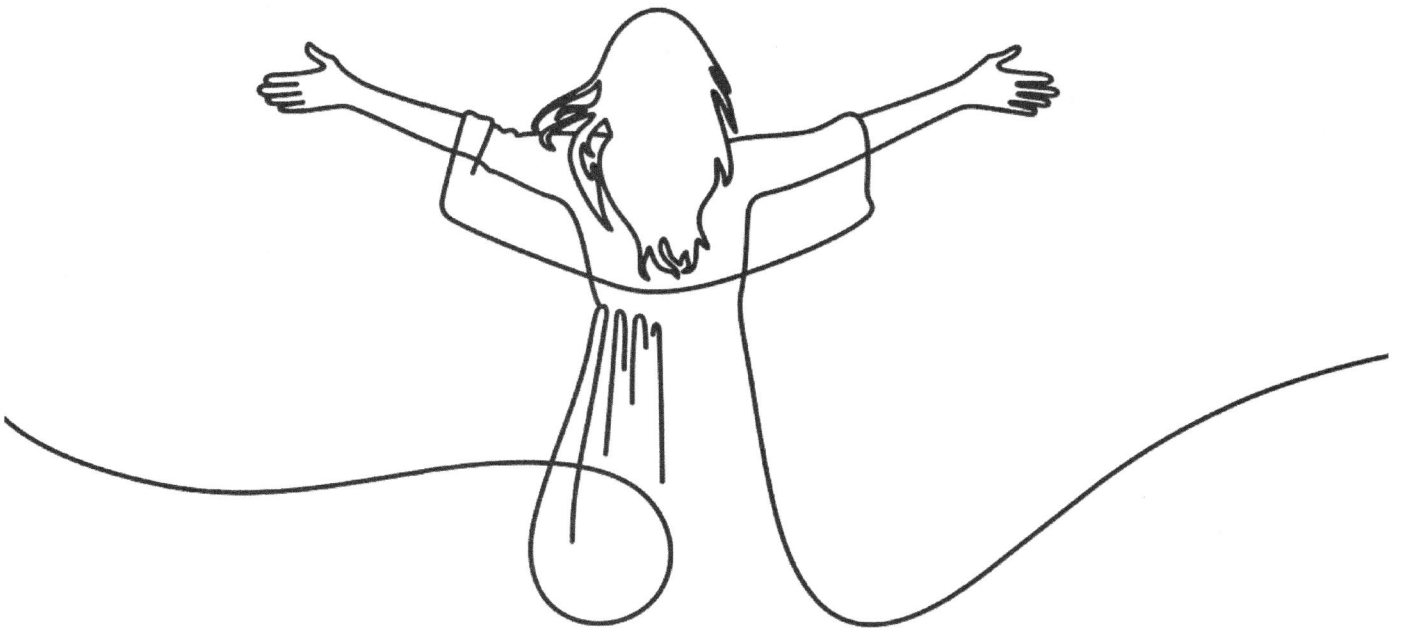

"LIFE IS NOT MEASURED BY THE NUMBER OF BREATHS WE TAKE, BUT BY THE MOMENTS THAT
TAKE OUR BREATH AWAY."
—MAYA ANGELOU, "BREATHLESS MOMENTS"

Blowing Dandelions

Leo was on a mission. My bright-eyed, 15-month-old grandson was resolute as together we walked through the park looking for fluffy dandelions. We spotted one just a few feet in front of us. With all the breath a two-and-a-half-foot tall toddler could muster, he bent down and blew the fuzzy white fluff out into the air. His vibrant smile reflected both satisfaction and delight. Then, "More…more!" he pleaded, in hopes of finding yet another. For about 20 minutes we searched the uneven grassy terrain. With each new dandelion we huffed and puffed and blew the fuzzy seed ball, dispersing the feather-light seeds into the air. Each new dandelion brought joy and laughter. It seemed as though Leo's curiosity and desire for more could not be satiated. Finally, not a single dried dandelion remained. I marveled at his focus and passion for discovery, as well as his enjoyment of such a common object in God's creation. Leo's delight brought great pleasure to my own heart.

As adults, our sense of wonder sometimes resembles childlike delight and curiosity about the world we live in. It can feel like deep gratitude as we appreciate the colorful beauty and scent of a single rose, or enjoy the majesty of a well-orchestrated symphony. We might stand in awe of the detailed plans for a new home that's being built, or a lovely herb garden that's being cultivated. An unforgettable train ride in Italy from Assisi to Orvieto, passing through Tuscany, comes to mind. I remember many miles of eye-popping views of golden sunflowers and bright red poppies that delighted my senses, birthing wonder and awe within me.

As we grow older, though, we too often become slaves to our work and get wrapped up in the worrisome responsibilities of life. Our sense of wonder is snuffed out like a candle in the wind. We miss out on the many benefits childlike wonder has to offer. We ignore the deep appreciation that births joy and feelings of well-being, and which in return increases our ability to be creative and productive. We deny the delight and gratitude that contribute to good physical, mental and emotional health. Gratitude can even help heal a broken heart. But if we're not careful, we can become so overwhelmed with meeting deadlines and accomplishing more that we become numb to the beauty and opportunities all around us.

So, how do we find or cultivate a sense of wonder and delight within ourselves?

Finding Delight And Wonder

For me, there's almost nothing quite like viewing an ever-changing sunset. The lively kaleidoscope of colors painted across the sky, like the brush strokes of a master painter, fascinated me Just last night as I sat having dinner with a friend. The experience was one of visual awe and fascination. That God continues to display unique versions of His creation is a mystery almost unfathomable. Sometimes we actually have to go looking for evidence of God's unique gifts, with eyes wide open and an expectant heart.

I have enjoyed meandering along nature paths, as I've done on many of our trips to Zion National Park in Utah. When I am intentional in my search for beauty, there is a greater probability that I will both find it and experience God's presence in some spectacular way. Perhaps I will be drawn to the vast grandeur of red Navajo sandstone cliffs surrounding me. From higher elevations I admire the rushing Virgin River flowing through a valley full of bright yellow aspen trees. At places where the water is more still, it becomes a mirror reflecting the mountainous landscape on its perimeter.

Engaging in the practices of noticing and being present allows me to stop and slow down long enough to drink in the beauty and uniqueness of my surroundings. Turning around slowly I feel grounded amidst a colorful majestic panoramic view. I am exhilarated by the joyful play of cloud formations being arranged and rearranged by wind gusts on a blustery day. Each experience is novel as I open myself to the remarkable wonder and mystery of every magical moment. My search for the wonder and awe has taken me to many countries around the globe, I have also found it in my own backyard, and other people's.

We can experience the gifts of wonder and awe by being intentional, and using the spiritual practices of noticing and being present.

I often experience awe and wonder through reading Scripture. Let's look through the eyes of the psalmist, who recognizes awe and wonder, as he recalls how God stills the seas, the roaring waves, and establishes the mountains. As you read through this Scripture passage slowly, several times, allow the truth of God's awesomeness to sink from your mind to your heart.

A Scripture Meditation On Wonder: Prayerfully Read, Reread, And Meditate

By awesome deeds You answer us with righteousness, O God of our salvation, the hope of all the ends of the earth and of the farthest seas; the One who by His strength established the mountains, being girded with might; who stills the roaring seas, the roaring of their waves, the tumult of the peoples, so that those who dwell at the ends of the earth are in awe at Your signs. You make the going out of the morning and the evening to shout for joy.
—Psalm 65:5-8, ESVUK

One of my favorite poets invites us to treat all of life as sacred, brimming with divine love.

Earth's crammed with heaven,

And every common bush afire with God; But only he who sees, takes off his shoes, The rest sit round it and pluck blackberries.
—Elizabeth Barrett Browning

The more we notice, immerse ourselves in, and appreciate the presence of God in nature the more easily wonder begins to burst upon us.

A Meditation On Child-Like Wonder[36]

Paraphrased from Lectio 365 App, Daily on-line devotional, 24-7 Prayer
Created by Pete Greig and 24-7 Prayer team members

Introduction

When was the last time you were seized by awe and wonder? Holy Spirit, would you bring to mind that memory? (Pause and reflect.)

If a memory comes to mind, hold it in your mind's eye and savor that moment of wonder.

Once again, the practice of *revisiting* helps us reclaim the wonder of God's presence in a past moment or event.

Perhaps nothing comes to mind. Consider these alternate questions:

1. God, I wonder where my wonder has gone?
2. Am I disappointed?
3. Have I become cynical?
4. Am I tired from work or worried?
5. Does wonder feel too vulnerable or childish?

Talk to God about this today.

Pause And Pray

"God, today I thank You for the children in my life. Guard their wide-eyed wonder, their ability to perceive the joy and beauty of life and to receive all your good gifts. I pray for myself, that I may never forget my First Love. You are the One who first filled my heart with the wonder of perfect love. Help me to always remember the vulnerability that led me to open up to Your presence and goodness. Help me, like a child, to walk with my eyes wide open to the wonder and mystery of who You are. Amen."

Read slowly through Ephesians 3:14-21 from The Passion Translation, noticing which words or phrases draw you toward a deeper understanding of God's awesomeness.

So, I kneel humbly in awe before the Father of our Lord Jesus, the Messiah, the perfect Father of every father and child in heaven and on the earth. And I pray that He would unveil within you the unlimited riches of His glory and favor until supernatural strength floods your innermost being with His divine might and explosive power. Then, by constantly using your faith, the life of Christ will be released deep inside you, and the resting place of His love will become the very source and root of your life.

Then you will be empowered to discover what every holy one experiences— the great magnitude of the astonishing love of Christ in all its dimensions. How deeply intimate and far-reaching is His love! How enduring and inclusive it is! Endless love beyond measurement that transcends our understanding—this extravagant love pours into you until you are filled to overflowing with the fullness of God!

Never doubt God's mighty power to work in you and accomplish all this. He will achieve infinitely more than your greatest request, your most unbelievable dream, and exceed your wildest imagination! He will outdo them all, for His miraculous power constantly energizes you.

Now, we offer up to God all the glorious praise that rises from every church in every generation through Jesus Christ—and all that will yet be manifest through time and eternity. Amen!

David Benner says that we cannot produce wonder. We can, however, be open to it and make space and room for awe.[37]

How can we make room today? How might our eyes be open to the majesty and awesomeness of God in His Word and His world, and in our lives?

Pause And Pray: A Yielding Prayer

"God, I confess to you my disappointment, weariness, and my cynicism.
I repent for a life so full of work and worry that there is little room for
wonder. Give me the eyes, the faith, the expectancy, and the joyfulness of
a child today. You are wonder-ful. May I be wonder-ful as well."

—Paraphrased from Lectio 365[38]

Notice the Psalmist's description of the ways God has created you "Wonder-fully."

For you created my inmost being;
you knit me together in my mother's womb.
I praise you because I am fearfully and wonderfully made;
your works are wonderful,
I know that full well.
My frame was not hidden from you
when I was made in the secret place,
when I was woven together in the depths of the earth.
Your eyes saw my unformed body;
all the days ordained for me were written in your book
before one of them came to be.
How precious to me are your thoughts, God!
How vast is the sum of them!
Were I to count them,

they would outnumber the grains of sand—

when I awake, I am still with you.

—Psalm 139:13-18

Spiritual Practices Can Lead Us To Wonder And Mystery

Spiritual practices are a critical part of our spiritual life, because they teach us how to "draw near" to God and how to open ourselves up, allowing God to do His work. Through the practices we create space for interior God-movement to occur. These moments may not always occur, and they may not happen in the ways we hope or expect. In other words, the practices are not bargaining chips: *"I'll read the Bible and pray so that God will let me go to Disneyland or Europe."* However, when we engage in spiritual practices, there is a higher likelihood that we will hear from God or experience His presence. Spiritual practices are a part of our training. They are tools to help us break through the barriers and the fears that separate us from God. It's God who is in control of the times and the ways He chooses to reveal Himself. This is part of what mystery is about: deciding to let God work in us in the way He thinks is best. Our part is to come with a trusting heart. Becoming more and more open handed and attentive to God's overtures of love toward us will, naturally, bring about in us movement toward His heart and a deeper knowing of Him in all His glory and wonder.

Some of the practices I've found especially helpful as I've grown in my awareness of mystery and wonder:

- slowing and noticing
- being fully present
- taking a long thoughtful look at the clouds
- nature walks
- revisiting
- silent meditation
- gratitude
- celebration
- communion

I've included a list of Prompts that Inspire a Grateful Heart and Ideas for Celebration on the following pages. It might be helpful to copy the list and put it in your Bible or in a place where you have alone time with God. Try choosing a new prompt each day and then begin again. I find that gratitude is one of the easiest ways of finding peace in a difficult season, or being uplifted when my mood is low and discouragement sets in.

Gratitude primes our hearts for wonder!

Prompts That Inspire A Grateful Heart

- **Pick out three things in your day that are beautiful**. Take time to notice and appreciate them in the moment. Then, jot them down or describe them in your journal.

- **Savor something**. Stay in the shower for a few seconds longer, or take a moment to appreciate the smell of your morning coffee before your first sip. Try to elongate the pleasant moments of your day, no matter how small.

- **Notice three good things**. Write down three things that went well in your day and *why* they went well. These don't have to be big things. Sometimes the smallest, seemingly insignificant things can have the greatest impact on your life.

- **Describe a life-giving situation.** Think of a moment today when you felt happy, loved, contented, peaceful, etc. What were you doing? How did the situation come to be? How did you feel (both emotionally and physically)? Use as many sensory details as you can.

- **Find something positive about today**. Take note of what this experience does to your body. What does it mean to actually *feel* happy? How does it affect how you breathe and move? Write about it.

- **What did you enjoy most today?** Write about it.

- **Gratitude list**. Write a list of the things you're grateful for. If you find that you list (mostly) the same things each time, pick different contexts to focus on: things about your family, things at work, things in the external world, etc.

- **What gives you a sense of wonder?** Looking up at the clouds, studying their shapes and movement; stargazing on a clear night; watching children play; strolling through an art gallery? Let a sense of childlike delight and wonder permeate your thoughts.

- **When and what gave you a sense of being loved, listened to, encouraged, comforted, or supported?** What did it reveal to you about God's character?

- **Create a list of activities that make you happy**. Then put a check mark next to the ones that you do on a regular basis. Try to incorporate these more frequently into your week.

Spiritual Practice: Celebration

God celebrates! He invented joy and celebration. The Old Testament is full of examples of Jewish celebrations. Jesus, Himself, after He broke bread with His disciples said, *"This is my body, which is given for you. Do this in remembrance of me"* (Luke 22:18-20). As Christians, we honor the gift of Jesus' death and resurrection by partaking in the celebration of communion. We can enter into God's presence through the practice of celebration. Whether solemn or exhilarating, formal or spontaneous, celebration can enlarge our capacity to enjoy and appreciate life and get in touch with the mystery and wonder of who God is. Celebration does not depend on perfect circumstances or happy feelings. Even in prison Paul and Silas found something to sing about.

> *About midnight Paul and Silas were praying and singing hymns to God, and the other prisoners were listening to them. Suddenly there was such a violent earthquake that the foundations of the prison were shaken. At once all the prison doors flew open, and everyone's chains were loose.*
> —Acts 16:26-27

Listen to the words of Jeremiah, the weeping prophet, expressing hope in the midst of sadness.

> *My soul is downcast within me. Yet this I call to mind and therefore I have Hope. Because of the LORD's great love, we are not consumed. For His compassions never fail. They are new every morning.*
> —*Lamentations 3:20-23a*

Whether we're having a great day or a challenging day, we can cultivate an attitude of gratitude and a heart full of wonder by celebrating defining moments. Celebration can also be a weekly event as we observe the Sabbath, a day set aside to focus on being present with God. Check out the examples of significant moments below. As you peruse this list, determine which ideas/events seem worthy of celebration. You may want to periodically design a whole day, a half day, or an evening of celebration as a way of highlighting something you are grateful for.

Significant Moments Worth Celebrating

We typically celebrate birthdays, holidays, graduations, and marriages as significant life events. However, there are many other events that may warrant a special day of joy or celebration. Setting aside time to celebrate enables us to enjoy life more fully. Choose one or more of the ideas below and add them to your calendar. One key to enhancing your celebration is entering in with all five senses. Slowly savor each aspect of your experience by noticing the tastes, sounds, smells, sights, and textures available to you.

- **Beauty** – We sit and watch a striking sunrise or sunset, delighting in the glorious display of intermingling bright yellows, pinks and oranges streaming across a painted sky. Beholding the soft delicate petals of a simple magenta rose, seeing the first steps of a six-month-old, who walks for the very first time, or hearing the *boom* of waves crashing in rhythmic motion along the shoreline can elicit within us a sense of wonder. Contemplative nature walks in forests rich with the sights and smells of evergreen trees can bring us to a place of joyful serenity. Choose your favorite or most available form of beauty.

- **Accomplishments** – We finish a challenging task or a job done well. We compete and excel at an athletic event. We finish writing our first book, pass an important exam, or receive recognition at work when we've clinched a big contract. We are selected to an honored position or for a specific role because of an area of expertise we have cultivated.

- **Beginnings and Endings** – We hear and respond to God's specific call on our lives. Then we go on to teach, empower, and serve others. Perhaps we are called to show kindness to the elderly, or work with children with special needs. New beginnings and endings can all prompt a well-deserved celebration.

- **Birth of a Child** – Nothing compares to the thrill surrounding the birth of a child. Looking into the tiny tender innocent face of a newborn reminds us that God is good and so are His gifts. This mystery is unfathomable.

- **Death as a Celebration of Life** – Honoring the life and death of a beloved friend or family member is sometimes called a celebration of life. Though the pain is palpable, God comforts us in our sorrow as we focus on the value of our loved one's life. Joy or gratitude can be experienced alongside the grief.

- **Consolations Without Previous Cause** – These are granted by God alone. St Ignatius of Loyola recognized that there are times when we experience the wonder, mystery, and presence of God without anything specific happening to bring it about. It is as though the heart and mind are filled with undeniable joy or love for no reason other than God's graciousness. Ignatius calls these moments "Consolations without Previous Cause," where the "Creator comes into the soul, to leave it, to act upon it, to draw it wholly to the love of the Divine."[39]

- **Sabbath Rest** – We choose to embrace a regular rhythm of setting aside one day a week to enjoy God's presence and recognize the body's need for rest and relaxation. It reminds us that our lives aren't just about doing and achieving. We let go of "have-to's" and experience the beauty of just being in God's loving presence through the things we enjoy. We can choose to feast, enjoy friends and family, or take a slow stroll by the lake as we celebrate His presence and goodness.

- **Celebrating for No Specific Reason** – Set aside a day to highlight something positive in your life, just because your soul needs it. Choose something to celebrate. See below for instructions.

When I was quite young, we would occasionally celebrate someone's "Unbirthday", by singing a song "A Very Merry Unbirthday", from Alice in Wonderland. We decorated, made a cake, and pretended it was a special day—just for fun!

Designing A Day Of Celebration

Over the years I've had lots of fun with the practice of celebration. Sometimes I celebrate God's beauty by planning a half-day alone at the beach, where I can simply enjoy God's presence using my five senses, opening my entire being to the beauty around me. Other times I've included friends or ministry partners, incorporating activities we can experience and reflect on together.

1. Determine what you'd like to celebrate "just because." It could be the end of your work week, the coming of spring (or any season), a special time with a friend or family member, or one of the significant moments listed above.
2. Determine the focus of the gathering. Will it simply be a social gathering or will it have a spiritual element, such as having a practice you engage in and process together?
3. Decide what activities you'd like to engage in to make the occasion special.
4. Set a time and a place to celebrate. Will you want to be out in nature, at a restaurant, in a cozy home, somewhere else?
5. Make a list of supplies, food, drinks, or other items you might need.
6. Send an invitation to those you want to include.
7. Solicit any help you might need.
8. Attend your celebration with a grateful heart, wearing clothes that are comfortable or appropriate for the occasion, fit well, and make you happy.

Reflections On The Practice

A celebration can be as simple as serving cake and ice cream at the end of a meeting to honor someone's accomplishment, enjoying a glass of wine and a plate of fruit to celebrate a friend's visit, or taking a plate of homemade brownies to honor a grandson's birthday.

At the end of each 10-week *Heart of the Journey* class, we enjoyed the practice of celebration. Small bottles of bubbles were purchased for each participant. After enjoying a table full of sweet and savory refreshments, we met outside and blew bubbles. As hundreds of bubbles floated above us, the scene was delightful. Smiles and spontaneous laughter were evidence of joy, as each graduate engaged in this fun familiar childhood activity.

Once you've participated in the practice of celebration, you might want to reflect on the following three questions:

1. Where did I experience feelings of joy, gratitude, or the peaceful presence of God?
2. In what ways did God seem to meet me during my practice?
3. What did I notice?
4. How was God present or not present?
5. What might I do differently to enhance my experience of God's presence through the practice of celebration?
6. Did I sense any resistance within myself to the practice of celebration?

_____

_____

_____

_____

_____

After blowing bubbles with Heart of the Journey participants, we gathered for a reflective discussion. Many noticed the light and easy way the bubbles floated upward around the church campus. It reminded them of the verses in Matthew 11:28-29, in which Jesus describes our walk with Him. In these verses Jesus calls the weary and burdened to His rest. He describes Himself as *"gentle and humble in heart"* and promises *"rest for your souls."* (His) *"yoke is easy and (His) burden is light."* The bubbles were the perfect picture of Jesus' personal invitation to each of us. They were also a reminder that:

> *It is never too late to enjoy your childhood, especially if you somehow missed the one you lived through.*

On the other hand, some participants felt a sense of resistance to blowing bubbles in public, perhaps feeling it was a bit too childish. We discussed resistance and how it can offer us clues about our struggles with the false self. Are we concerned with image management and what others think of us? Are we afraid to take risks? Do we lack the freedom to just "be"? And how do these things get in the way of our intimacy with God and others? Try blowing bubbles yourself, or with a group of children. Reflect on your experience

A Word On Mystery

We've spent a good amount of time talking about methods and how-to's in this book. We've looked at spiritual practices, and some of the ways God shows up for us as we discern His presence. Another avenue for God's transformational work in us comes from how we meet God in the everyday happenings of life such as relationships, suffering, and woundedness. The fact that God is present in our times of loss, betrayal, grief, tragedy, and trauma is more about mystery than it is about mastery of practices or concepts. At the core of all of this, the heart of our journey is an ever-growing relationship of intimacy with God. There is no exact method or formula to be learned. It is more about an attitude of heart and mind; a quiet openness and availability to surrender to God. As we wait for, trust in, and walk in the knowledge of His abiding presence with us, He meets us in unexpected ways.

Just as God met me in the midst of losing my first child, so many years ago, God can meet us in the midst of our grieving and sadness. Our sorrow-laden spirits can be replaced with hope and joy in a way that only God can do. This joy is a gift from Him, though we may have done nothing to cause it to happen. God grants us the faith to believe that He is here with us; whether or not we feel His presence, whether or not we experience some tangible evidence of His personhood. This is a mystery and wonder. As we continue to lean into the heart of our First Love, we are at home with Him in our hearts. And He is at home within us.

Nine Ways We Cultivate Intimacy With God By Opening To Mystery

Practice cultivating a heart of surrender by giving the control of your life to God. It may seem to some like a daunting task. The *Welcoming Prayer,* as taught by Thomas Keating, can help us let go and surrender. It may take some practice to begin to live into this prayer. Our psyche (our mind— both conscious and unconscious) is use to wanting its own way. The Welcoming Prayer helps us let go of having to have our own way and surrendering to God's presence and action in our lives.

We pray the Welcoming Prayer slowly and thoughtfully.[40]

The Welcoming Prayer

Welcome, welcome, welcome.
I welcome everything that comes to me today, because I know it's for my healing.
I welcome all thoughts, feelings, emotions, persons, situations, and conditions.
I let go of my desire for power and control.
I let go of my desire for affection, esteem, approval, and pleasure.
I let go of my desire for survival and security.
I let go of my desire to change any situation, condition, person, or myself.
I open to the love and presence of God and God's action within. Amen.
—The Welcoming Prayer created by Mary Mrozowski in 2017, taught by Thomas
Keating on the podcast "Practice for Daily Life: The Welcoming Prayer," The
Contemplative Dimension of the Twelve Steps with Thomas Keating, Part 1.

Sitting silently in God's presence and simply focusing on Him can also help us relinquish our need for control. This is something you'll probably have to grow into, if it isn't already a part of your time with God. Most of us experience the "monkey mind": thoughts that race in and out whenever we try to be still enough to pray, meditate, or sit silently in God's presence. It's been suggested that as we practice silence, we imagine a river running before us. As thoughts, emotions, or objects come into our mind, we let them float on by, as the steady stream of water washes them down stream.

Become aware of the ways God is already working in your life and join Him in that process or activity. The Prayer of Examen has helped me see where God is most active in my life.

Stop and reflect on your day so far. Consider the following two questions from the Prayer of Examen. They can help pinpoint ways God has shown up and is active in your life. It can become the basis of a mini-celebration.

> *"What made me feel most loved/ joyful/ peaceful today?"* (List 1-3 things)
>
> *"When or about what did I sense a heart of gratitude today?"*

_____

_____

_____

_____

Look deeply into your thoughts and feelings for clues to how and where God was most present in your day.

Pause and savor the answers. Delight in God's goodness.

Respond to God from a place of *already* knowing your identity in Him. In other words, train yourself to speak words that affirm God's faithfulness, love, and care for you because you know they are true, even when you don't necessarily feel them. You may first need to ground yourself in specific characteristics of your beloved-ness if you tend to have doubts. For example, remind yourself of who you truly are by repeating out loud one or more of the statements below:

- I am loved and God rejoices over me. (Zephaniah 3:17, ESV)
- I have been chosen and adopted into God's family. (2 Thessalonians 2:13, Galatians 4:5, Ephesians 1:4-5)
- I have already been forgiven. (Micah 7:18, Isaiah 53:6)
- I have been fearfully and wonderfully made. (Psalms 139:14)
- I have been appointed to bear fruit. (John 15:16)
- I am complete through union with Him. (Colossians 2:10)
- I have authority to overcome. (Luke 9:1, Matthew 10:1)
- I am called according to His purpose and am worthy of that calling. (Romans 8:28, Ephesians 4:1)

Pay attention to God's promptings throughout your day. In the midst of the normal flow of the day you may sense a gentle prompting. It might seem like a quiet, subtle thought that has some weight or importance to it. Sometimes I get a gentle prompting to text someone an encouraging word or a message of gratitude. When I act on these promptings, feelings of pleasure and joy emerge within me. There is a sense of God using me, partnering with me, or of me partnering with Him. Obedience to God's voice/promptings is one of the ways we sense His delight and experience intimacy with Him.

Practice paying attention to how God shows up through the acts of kindness of friends and family. It's easy to take small acts of kindness and even relationships for granted. Last week a friend brought me a bouquet of flowers. Another friend gave me a fresh-baked loaf of sourdough bread. Allow people to be themselves and take notice when they bless you with specific loving acts, gestures, or words. Even a smile can remind us of the way God delights in us and sees us as the *"apple of His eye"* (Psalm 17:8 and Deuteronomy 32:10).

Spend time in conversation with God either orally or in writing. Listen for His responses and respond back. Listening will be the most challenging part. When I take time to pause and listen for God's response, His comforting words, like *"I am here with you,"* wash over me as a gentle reminder. My soul sinks with delight into the mystery of God's *"I-am-with-you-always"* presence.

Meditate on the beauty of God as seen in creation or works of art. Our back yard is graced with a variety of colorful flowering plants, which bring joy to my soul as I gaze out my kitchen window while making my morning coffee. This sneak peek of God's glory greets and delights me each morning. I have a fondness for works of art. We've collected wall art from several countries while on pilgrimage. Each of these was specially chosen to delight our souls and our senses.

Intentionally make space in your life for silence and solitude, where you let your thoughts constantly return to God. Teach your mind to dwell on Him when you are alone. Refrain from filling every moment with something to do or accomplish. Allow yourself to simply be loved by the one who first loved you.

And whatever you do, don't forget to play. It's a lost art form for many adults. There is so much joy we can experience when we step aside from all the comings and goings and doing of everyday life. When I first wrote the story of Leo blowing dandelions, he was only fifteen months old. Now, as I finalize this book with the last remaining strokes on my keyboard, Leo, short for Leonardo, is two years and six months old. A new little baby brother has been born. Enzo, short for Lorenzo, brings with him the promise of double the opportunities for play, laughter and enjoyment. My weekly time with them is one of the highlights of my week. My two older grandsons provide additional opportunities for play and enjoyment, as we spend time together walking on the beach, cooking in the kitchen, or swimming in our backyard pool. Grandchildren are often a source of much pleasure and delight.

Extending The Learning

We can continue to grow in our experience of Wonder and Mystery by using some of the strategies above. In doing this we are training our minds, emotions, and bodies to experience more of God's goodness and to respond to Him with a grateful heart. Here are a few more ideas. You might want to copy these in your journal or put a list of them in your Bible for easy access.

• Praising God	• Giving thanks and showing gratitude
• Creating something	• Looking for beauty in small things
• Showing appreciation	• Looking for God's movement in your life
• Being still	• Sharing intimately in a safe environment
• Taking nature walks	• Letting go of what isn't working
• Serving others	• Taking care of yourself
• Encouraging someone	• Revisiting (reimagining) beautiful moments
• Listening well to someone	• Meditating on what's life-giving
• Forgiving yourself and others	• Sharing a meal with good friends and family
• Not comparing	• Listening to beautiful music
• Worshiping	• Dancing as a praise offering to God
• Leaning into God's love	• Blowing bubbles or dandelions
• Cultivating community	

Nuggets For The Journey

Worship as Meditation

I love the way the beautiful worship song from Hillsong, "So Will I," expresses wonder and delight by showcasing God's greatness and majesty, as well as how nature responds in adoration of who God is. You might want to download the words and melody of this song and play it two or three times while meditating on the words and messages.

As you listen, ask yourself:

- Which lines or phrases seem to carry the most weight or meaning and why?

- What qualities of God's character are you most drawn to through this song?

- What additional songs or Scripture verses usually help you see and understand more of how God is wonder-ful?

In his book *Life Without Lack*, Dallas Willard quotes Paternus' *"Advice to a Son."* It gives us several clues to how we can live life in the fullness, wonder, and awe of God's presence.

First of all, my child, think magnificently of God.
Magnify Him, adore His power,
pray to Him frequently and incessantly.
Bear Him always in your mind.
Teach your thoughts to reverence Him in every place,
for there is no place where He is not.
Therefore, my child, fear and worship and love God;
first and last, think magnificently of Him.[41]

Bringing It All Together

If you've made it to the end of this book, kudos to you!

It is my hope and prayer that throughout your reading you have experienced hope and increased intimacy with our Creator.

This happens as we learn to linger with Him, attuned to His beautiful presence; allowing ourselves to rest "under the shelter of his wings." With His gentle loving arms and infinite love He reaches out, offering more of Himself; all the while loving us into wholeness.

This is not a one-and-done type of thing. The invitation is to a life-long, walk-along-side kind of journey, as we sit in the Presence, take the hand of the Master, and moment by moment trust in the One who has led you to this point.

Through this intentional relational connection, as we attune to His presence, our Creator will make himself known to us. *"You make known to me the path of life;You will fill me with joy in Your presence..."* (Psalm 16:11)

Tips For The Trail

Here are some reminders of what we've shared together on this path toward encountering Jesus and joining Him as He forms us to become more like the Master. You may even want to copy these and insert them into your Bible or journal, as gentle reminders on this ever winding trail.
Spiritual Practices are medicine for our soul, as they help encourage, calm, and enlighten us. Spiritual Practices are one of the gateways to developing intimacy with God, which is the point of this book.
Trust the Spirit to give you wisdom to discern which practices are best for us in this current season of our lives. Start with one. Add another when you are ready. Discern what excess commitments to let go of to make room for enjoying creative moments of connections with the Divine.
Take some time to think and reflect on what practice speaks to your heart. Ask for the Spirit's leading in how to best continue your transformation journey.

Never allow shame to dictate who you think you are. Instead, trust in the truth of Scripture, which reveals your true identity as the beloved of God, created for joy, and destined for glory.

Be honest with yourself about your weaknesses and receive professional help with the deeper issues of your life that hold you back or block you from receiving peace.

Stay connected to Jesus. As you awake each morning, see His face with the eyes of your imagination; noticing Him smiling back at you.

We were created for connection. Find a safe community, one in which you feel loved and accepted as you are, and where you can share the pain and pleasures of life.

Develop a relationship with someone who embodies spiritual wisdom and in whom you can share openly and honestly. A counselor, spiritual director or Emmanual Prayer practitioner can be helpful throughout the process of getting to know yourself and God.

Engage in the practices of thanksgiving and revisiting. Re-imagine a special memory, caring person, or beautiful experience in nature, and be thankful for these. Express gratitude to those around you and to God himself often.

Guard your heart and mind. It can be a scary thought, but we tend to become like what we most often think about. *"Whatever is true, whatever is honorable, whatever is just, whatever is pure, whatever is lovely, whatever is commendable, if there is any excellence, if there is anything worthy of praise, think about these things.* –Philippians 4:8

And finally, may you lean into the tender passionate heart of the Divine Healer of your soul.

Now I would like to share one last story with you.

This week a friend reminded me of a time, many years ago, when we were attending a Dallas Willard seminar. Dallas had been my mentor and hero "from afar", and I traveled to hear him speak whenever I could. After the presentation he invited up any who had a personal question they wanted to ask. A long line formed down the center aisle of the church, and I was the very last person. Slowly, one by one, folks got their questions answered. Finally, it was my turn.

 Rather nervously, I asked, "Is there a curriculum written for churches that we could use to help groups of seekers on this Spiritual Formation pathway?" These were the early years, and I knew of no such thing. "No," he replied thoughtfully. "You'll have to write it yourself."

This was not the answer I was hoping for, but it did add fuel to the fire of my passion to write the original outline for the *Heart of the Journey* class and to teach it for over ten years to hundreds of participants. Since then, many books have been written and classes taught. I am grateful for God's prompting me, through Dallas, to pen my personal "Journey into the Heart of God."

I am hopeful that it was life-changing for you as you read, and that you will continue to grow into a person of joy, who lives out the purpose for which God has designed you as – *His Masterpiece.*

APPENDIX A

PRACTICES AS THEY APPEAR IN THIS BOOK

Chapter 1: Journaling (As A Listening Activity), Devotional Reading

Chapter 2: Breath Prayer, Slowly, Noticing

Chapter 3: Self-Examination, Confession

Chapter 4: Prayer (As Being, Waiting, Listening, And Responding), Visio Divina

Chapter 5: Imaginative Prayer

Chapter 6: Prayer (As Listening, Disclosing, Absorbing, Reflecting, Responding, And Giving)

Chapter 7: Lectio Divina

Chapter 8: Preparation For Forgiveness

Chapter 9: Forgiveness, Self-Examination, Gratitude

Chapter 10: Revisiting, Developing A Rhythm/Rule Of Life

Chapter 11: Gratitude, Day Of Celebration, Opening To Wonder

APPENDIX B

LIVING INTENTIONALLY SURVEY

Questions To Help You Update Or Revise Your Rule Of Life

How would I describe the relationship with God that I desire and seek?

What spiritual practices do I already know positively feed this relationship?

What practices might I adopt that would help me grow in this relationship?

What pattern or rhythm of practices would actually fit my present circumstances?

To which relationships in my life would I like to give special attention?

In what ways can I contribute to the work of God in the world, advancing the cause of peace and justice and bringing healing, reconciliation, and hope to my community, my church, my nation, and the world?

Where in my relationship with myself do I recognize the need for change or balance, and how can I incorporate "soul care" or "self-care" (healthy eating, exercise, sleep, creativity, rest, recreation) into my rhythm?

How can I be a good steward of the resources God has entrusted to me (money, possessions, talents, time education, experience, etc.

How can I care for the environment (e.g. by living more simply and avoiding wasteful extravagance)?

What commitment am I sensing I'd like to make to God and to the church or another group regarding my talents, time, and resources?

How can I be more intentional in taking responsibility for my ongoing spiritual growth?

WITH GRATITUDE

We are happiest when our hearts and minds are full of gratitude. Looking back on the years of planning, preparing, writing, teaching, and finally, publishing this book, my heart is full. So many have contributed to each phase of the process. I am appreciative of each gift of your time and talents.

Beth Slevcove – For your encouragement and guidance in matters of the heart. Your enthusiasm for my initial vision helped sustain me as I wrote.

Rikah Thomas – For being instrumental in getting me started and being my cheerleader throughout this process. Your technical support was invaluable.

Jennevieve La Haye – For your over and above efforts to make the text more readable, the pictures suitable, and the Scripture references accurate. Your attention to detail was amazing. You were a true companion on this journey.

Damian Ludwig – For your artistic design talents in working with such a wide variety of projects related to this book: the cover, postcards, and my website. I am grateful for our gentle, collaborative discussions, which led to making the vision come alive with beauty and color.

Anne and Ron Richardson – For your consistent prayers, and detailed tips on writing and publishing. And especially Anne, who's encouragement never let me forget that creating this book was not just a possibility, but a Divine calling.

My Beta Readers – Anne, Barbara, ElRoy Jennevieve, Linda, Mark, and Tom for your time spent and for providing both encouragement and constructive ideas.

My Writing Group – Rikah, Anne, Julie, Corrine, Charlene, Cheri, and Tiffany for the much-needed advice on my personal stories. I grew in confidence as a writer through our critique sessions.

Sarah Hauge, my editor, for the many hours of collaboration and your detailed work on the book contents, ensuring this would be a professional product. You were a pleasure to work with.

My Spiritual Formation Group – Jennevieve, Jeremy, Kathryn, Damian, Cynthia, Christine, Kevin, and ElRoy for your prayers, partnership, camaraderie, and support in all things "Formation" over the years.

Heidi Saulsbury – For helping me fine-tune my stories and my purpose.

Ian Saulsbury – For the spontaneous photoshoot sessions.

ElRoy, my husband – For faithfully supporting me through two years of writing this book and through the 10 years of teaching and leading Heart of the Journey class together. You have done more dishes, made more shopping trips, and created more healthy meals than I could ever count… and all with a great attitude.

Journey Community Church – you provided the venue and the opportunity for the Heart of the

Journey class to thrive for over 10 years. God initiated the writing of the class, but you, as eager learners, happily filled our classes year after year. You provided the opportunity for each of the chapters to come alive, when they were only outlines for teaching.

Special thanks to Pastor Ed and Linda Noble and Ann and Butch Whitely. I am forever grateful for the many times you encouraged and supported us throughout the teaching of Heart of the Journey class, which eventually gave birth to the writing of this book.

And last, but definitely not least:

> *I will give thanks to You, O Lord, among the peoples. I will sing praises to you among the nations. For Your loving kindness is great to the heavens and Your truth to the clouds. Be exalted above the heavens, O God; let Your glory be above all the earth.*
> *—Psalm 5:9-11*

ABOUT THE AUTHOR

Beverly Peterson

Beverly Peterson has a passion for creating interactive opportunities for people to explore hearing God and experiencing His love more fully. It was out of her personal relationship and experiences with God that she wrote the curriculum for the Heart of the Journey class, which she and her husband taught for over 10 years at their local church. The core message of this ten-week class focused on developing an intimate relationship with Jesus resulting in a heart and mind spiritually transformed into His image.

Hundreds of participants successfully completed the class, many taking it more than once. They were encouraged to engage in spiritual practices that would allow them to make space to listen for God's voice and draw closer to Him. The results of this class were so favorable that the class content now exists in this book.

Beverly is a certificated spiritual director and has offered spiritual direction for the past 18 years. For the past 25 years she has written, taught classes, and led retreats focusing on spiritual formation and the contemplative tradition. In an earlier career, Beverly taught students in grades kindergarten through sixth grade for thirty-five years. She holds a lifetime teaching certificate and a master's degree in educational administration.

Part of Beverly's training in spiritual formation included seven spiritual pilgrimages to locations where past significant, sacred events had occurred. These pilgrimages included visits to a wide variety of cities throughout Italy and Spain. Additional pilgrimages took her to France, Switzerland, and the British Isles, including the Holy Isles of Iona and Lindisfarne, and finally two trips to Israel. While on pilgrimage, her desire was to meet God in iconic locations where the veil between heaven and earth seemed so thin that one's soul could almost touch heaven's glory.

Beverly and her husband live in San Diego, California, close enough to spend quality time with their adult, married children and four delightfully energetic grandsons. When she is not writing, Beverly enjoys walking barefoot on the beach, spending time with friends, blowing bubbles and dandelions with her youngest grandsons, and slowly sipping a warm cappuccino, preferably in Italy.

ENDNOTES

[1] Richard J. Foster, *Celebration of Discipline: The Path to Spiritual Growth* (San Francisco, CA: HarperSanFrancisco, 1978).

[2] Robert Mulholland, *Invitation to a Journey: A Road Map for Spiritual Formation*, Rev. ed. (Downers Grove, IL: InterVarsity Press, 2016).

[3] Adele Ahlberg Calhoun, *Spiritual Disciplines Handbook: Spiritual Practices That Transform Us* (Lisle, IL: InterVarsity Press, 2015), 167.

[4] Catherine of Siena, as cited in *The Lion Book of Famous Prayers: A Treasury of Christian Prayers Through the Centuries*, comp. Veronica Zundel (Oxford: Lion Publishing, 1983).

[5] Paul Steeves, *Getting to Know God* (Downers Grove, IL: InterVarsity Press, 1973).

[6] *Spiritual Disciplines Handbook: Practices That Transform Us, Rev. and expanded ed. (Downers Grove, IL: InterVarsity Press, 2015).*

[7] Ibid.

[8] Richard Rohr, "Creating God in Our Own Image," adapted from *Richard Rohr's Daily Meditations* (Franciscan Media, 2019).

[9] As quoted in sermons by Rev. Nathaniel Mahlberg, *The Dandelion Way* (blog), August 5, 2018.

[10] Richard Rohr, *The Universal Christ: How a Forgotten Reality Can Change Everything We See, Hope For, and Believe* (New York: Convergent Books, 2021).

[11] *Enfolded in Love: Daily Readings with Julian of Norwich,* ed. Robert Llewelyn (New York: HarperCollins, 1980).

[12] Thomas à Kempis, *Imitation of Christ*, trans. Aloysius Croft and Harold Bolton (Milwaukee, WI: The Bruce Publishing Company, 1940).

[13] Ibid.

[14] Augustine of Hippo, *Confessions*, written in Latin between AD 397-400.

[15] John Calvin, *Institutes of the Christian Religion: The Four Books Complete and Unabridged*, trans. Thomas Norton (Pantianos Classics, first published in English 1581).

[16] John Mark Comer, *The Ruthless Elimination of Hurry* (Colorado Springs, CO: WaterBrook, 2019).

[17] Zephaniah 3:17 paraphrased by Dennis Jernigan, as seen in "I Delight in You," *All In All Church, Teachings*, April 10, 2019. https://allinallchurch.com/teachings/4/10/i-delight-in-you.

[18] Classically Christian, "St. Catherine of Siena: 'Eternal Trinity, You Are a Deep Sea,'" April 29, 2016.

[19] Hafiz, "It Felt Love," *In Search of Starlight* (blog), by Dhruv Rajashekaran, December 7, 2014, https://insearchofstarlight.wordpress.com/2014/12/07/it-felt-like-love-hafiz-13th-century-persian-sufi-poet.

[20] John Stott, *The Radical Disciple: Some Neglected Aspects of Our Calling* (Downers Grove, IL: IVP Books, 2010).

[21] Dallas Willard, The Great Omission: Reclaiming Jesus' Essential Teachings on Discipleship (New York: HarperOne An Imprint of HarperCollins Publishers, 2006).

[22] Dallas Willard, *The Great Omission: Reclaiming Jesus' Essential Teachings on Discipleship* (New York: HarperOne, 2006), as reprinted in *Cutting Edge* magazine, Winter 2001.

[23] Gary L Thomas, *Sacred Pathways* (Grand Rapids, MI: Zondervan Books, 1996).

[24] Ibid.

[25] Mike Flynn and Doug Gregg, *Inner Healing: A Handbook for Helping Yourself and Others* (New York:

InterVarsity Press, 1993).

[26] Calhoun, *Spiritual Disciplines Handbook*.

[27] Ibid.

[28] St. Teresa of Avila, Spanish Carmelite nun and mystic (1515–1582).

[29] Dallas Willard, as reported by John Mark Comer in *The Ruthless Elimination of Hurry* (Colorado Springs, CO: WaterBrook, 2019), 18-19.

[30] Wayne Muller, *Legacy of the Heart: The Spiritual Advantages of a Painful Childhood* (New York: Simon & Schuster, 1992).

[31] This list comes from Robert S. McGee, *Searching for Peace* (Merritt Island, FL: Search Resources, 2003).

[32] This is the motto of navigator and sailor Sir Francis Drake.

[33] Julian of Norwich, 14th-century Christian mystic, as incorporated in T.S. Eliot's "Little Gidding," part four of *Four Quartets* (1943).

[34] McGee, *Searching for Peace*.

[35] Ruth Barton, *Sacred Rhythms: Arranging Our Lives for Spiritual Transformation* (Downers Grove, IL: InterVarsity Press, 2006).

[36] Paraphrased from *Lectio 365* app, daily devotional by 24-7 Prayer, created by Pete Greig and team members, available on the App Store.

[37] David G. Benner, *Soulful Spirituality: Becoming Fully Alive and Deeply Human* (Grand Rapids, MI: Brazos Press, 2011).

[38] Paraphrased from *Lectio 365* app, daily devotional by 24-7 Prayer, created by Pete Greig and team members, available on the App Store.

[39] Ignatian Spirituality, Ignatius of Loyola, as quoted in *Discernment for the Postmodern Condition*, by William Walson, September 11, 2019.

[40] The Welcoming Prayer, created by Mary Mrozowski in 2017, taught by Thomas Keating on the podcast *Practice for Daily Life: The Welcoming Prayer*, part of *The Contemplative Dimension of the Twelve Steps*.

[41] Dallas Willard, *Life Without Lack: Living in the Fullness of Psalm 23* (Nashville: Nelson Books, 2018).

Made in the USA
Las Vegas, NV
15 February 2025

17607665R00103